YACHT DESIGN DETAILS

OTHER BOOKS BY ROGER MARSHALL

A SAILOR'S GUIDE TO PRODUCTION SAILBOATS

DESIGNED TO CRUISE

RACE TO WIN

DESIGNED TO WIN

YACHT DESIGN

D E T A I L S

ROGER MARSHALL

HEARST MARINE BOOKS NEW YORK

Library of Congress Cataloging-in-Publication Data

Marshall, Roger.
    Yacht design details / Roger Marshall.
       p.   cm.
    ISBN 0-688-07215-1
    1. Yachts and yachting—Design and construction.   I. Title.
VM331.M374   1989
623.8′2023—dc19   88-38548
                                          CIP

Printed in the United States of America

First Edition

1 2 3 4 5 6 7 8 9 10

BOOK DESIGN BY JAYE ZIMET

CONTENTS

5

CONTENTS

CONTENTS

CONTENTS

CONTENTS

CHAPTER 7

DAVITS AND DINGHIES   155

INTRODUCTION

Most sailors who have owned their own boat for a few years want to make some changes in it. Often these changes are small, such as adding a table beside a bunk or adding an extra pad eye to make sail sheeting easier. Unfortunately, although most people know exactly what they want, they lack the knowledge to make the change themselves. They can always have the work done by a boatyard, of course, but boatyard work can be costly. There is also no guarantee that the yard will produce exactly what the owner has in mind. This book helps boat owners solve this problem by giving them the information they need to get the job done right. The handyman can use the drawings in these pages to make a new fitting himself, while the unhandy sailor can say to the yard, "Here is a picture of exactly what I want and I want it right here."

If you are not sure which category you fall into—handy or unhandy—you should take a few minutes to look through the drawings and explanations. You will find that most of the changes are reasonably easy to make. The average woodworker can make many of them over the winter and add them to the boat in the spring. There are smaller projects that you can start with and larger ones to which you can graduate as you gain experience, confidence, and skill. In the end you may be surprised at what you are able to accomplish.

The materials used in making a boat are seldom inexpensive, and your time is valuable, so be sure to measure everything carefully before cutting. As my old teacher used to say, measure twice, cut once. Make sure that new fittings will fit in the space available. There is nothing more frustrating than to have spent hours working on a special part only to find it is a fraction larger than the space it should fit in or a little too small to fill a gap. If you are adding an item with a door, for example, make sure the door has space to open and can be easily reached. If the door is hard to open, it will probably not be used.

Finally, while I have made every effort to ensure that the drawings are perfectly clear and that pieces fit together easily, I am working in two dimensions and your job is in three dimensions. It is not always possible to envision all the angles, and errors can creep in. Neither I nor the publisher can be held accountable for any errors. I can only urge you to think through the project carefully, check the drawings, check your measurements, and make corrections as required. If you do find an error, I hope you will let me know so that it can be eliminated in future editions. Good luck and have fun.

Roger Marshall
Jamestown, R.I.

HOW YOUR BOAT IS BUILT

If you are going to make changes to your boat, then it is imperative that you know approximately how the boat is built. Modern fiberglass production boats are built in a manner very different from that of a custom wooden boat. In this chapter we'll discuss the specifics of boat construction and where changes can easily be made. There are four basic methods of construction. They are:

- Modern production hulls
- Older production hulls
- Custom wooden boats
- Custom metal boats

Each has its own quirks and problems, especially when retrofitting or rebuilding is being considered. For instance, suppose we were going to install a simple locker against the hull and next to a bulkhead in each of these craft. In the production fiberglass hull we would have to remove the trim and any hull carpeting or ceiling, cut out the hull liner, trim the edges carefully, and glass the locker into the space. The locker would probably be built outside the boat and fitted carefully in place. Because it is being glassed to the hull, the locker can be of almost any size.

On the older production boat the job would be easier in that the trim would be made to be removed. Extraneous material can be cut away and the locker glassed into place.

A wooden boat presents a different set of problems in that the locker would probably be built on the boat and each part glued and screwed into place. It would be easy to screw new side pieces to an existing frame, but this would tend to restrict the size of the locker to one that would fit between the frames. Gluing and screwing would not work on a metal boat, however. Here the complete unit may be built outside the yacht and bolted through the metal frames to hold it in place, or it would be built on board and bolted through the frames. This means that the size of the locker would be governed by the distance between frames. These examples give you an idea how the method of construction of the boat affects the changes that may be made. Note also that in some cases the lockers can be built in the shop and simply added to the vessel, whereas sometimes it is easier to build the locker in the boat and offer it up to the work for fitting.

MODERN PRODUCTION BUILDING

If you bought a boat in the last ten years, the boat was probably constructed using some of the techniques developed to minimize costs and use fiberglass to its highest potential.

Today's production boats are built in a factory, often miles away from the ocean, and construction techniques are rarely geared to add-on items or retrofitting. The manufacturer, hopefully, includes most of the basics and then adds a list of options for you, as a buyer, to choose from. These options are then built in as the vessel is constructed. But, quite often, after you have sailed the boat for a while or after the warranty expires, your needs change or you find that small adjustments and additions are needed. This leaves you to make the changes or additions. But these changes can be difficult and sometimes horrendously expensive if you do not know how the boat was originally constructed. For instance, a client of my company wanted to add another winch to the deck of his boat. A simple enough procedure, he thought. He bought a winch, placed it on the boat where he thought it should go, marked out the position of the bolt holes, and proceeded to drill. He drilled the holes for the new winch and started to bolt it

into place. As the bolts were tightened, they gradually vanished into the overhead. At that point he called us.

We checked it over and found that he'd placed the winch in an area where low-density foam had been used as a core material. By tightening the bolts, he crushed the foam and weakened the structure. Eventually he had to get the yard to remove a section of the overhead, replace the core with a structurally stronger core, in this case plywood, and bolt the winch back into place with a backing plate to spread the load. If he'd added a backing plate initially, he would probably not have crushed the core and would have saved himself several hundred dollars in repair costs.

HULL CONSTRUCTION

A sailing yacht's hull is a relatively simple structure. It is generally made of hand-laid fiberglass held together with layers of polyester resin. The glass content will vary with the manufacturer, but is generally in the area of 35 to 40 percent of the total hull weight.

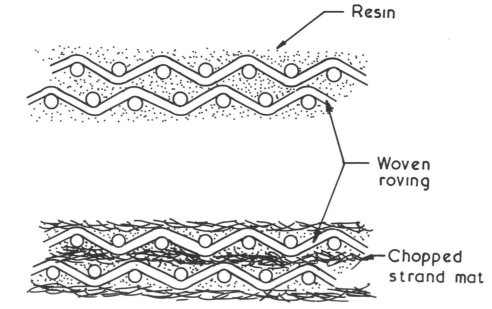

Resin

Woven roving

Chopped strand mat

F I G U R E 1

A laminate is usually made up with alternating layers of woven roving and chopped-strand mat. The resin fills the voids between the layers.

The hull is usually made from alternate layers of chopped-strand mat and woven rovings. The reason for this is shown in Figure 1. If two layers of woven roving are put next to each other, then there may be large areas filled with resin between the layers. This reduces the glass content of the laminate and makes it weaker. If two layers of chopped-strand mat are placed next to each other, the mat has little structural strength and the entire laminate may be weak. Chopped-strand mat is composed of short lengths of glass filaments that vary from 1 to 3 inches (25 mm to 75 mm). Woven roving is a loose-weave cloth formed by weaving the glass filaments into cloth. In the United States it comes in rolls 36 inches (914 mm) wide and in weights from 6 ounces to 24 ounces (170 grams to 680 grams). In Europe both woven roving and chopped strand mat are measured in grams per meter. Unidirectional cloth is made by laying long filaments in one direction, say north and south, and binding them with a light bonding of resin across the east-west direction. This is used where great strength is required in one direction only.

When a hull for a production boat is made, the first step is to polish the inside of the female mold. Then a mold-release wax is applied to ensure that the hull pops out of the mold easily. The next step is the gel coat. This is simply a layer of resin, often with a UV blocking agent added. Because of problems with hull blistering many manufacturers now use vinylester or Isophthalic resins in the gel coat rather than orphthothalic polyester resins. After the gel coat a light cloth, usually 4- or 6-ounce (100 gm/m² or 160 gm/m²) material is applied. (Note that chopped-strand mat is sold in ounces per square foot, so you will see numbers of ¾ to 3-ounce (18 gm/m² to 78 gm/m²) chopped-strand mat. Woven rovings are sold in ounces per square yard, so these numbers will be in the range of 6- to 24-ounce roving (160 gm/m² to 620 gm/m²). Metric sizes are shown in grams per square meter.) This is backed with a layer of chopped strand. The light cloth is used to prevent "print through." Print through means the weaving of the cloth can be seen through the gel coat and is a condition that may happen if a heavyweight cloth is used behind the gel coat.

Once these steps are finished, the laminate is built up in layers until the desired thickness and strength are reached. The laminate will generally be thicker toward the bottom as greater loads are imposed on the hull.

Many hulls are sandwich-cored. That is, they have a ½- or ¾-inch (12 mm or 18 mm) layer of balsa or foam between two laminates of fiberglass. This method increases the structural rigidity of the laminate without increasing the weight. The types of foam most often used are known by their trade names—Airex™, Klegecell™, Plasticell™, Termanto™, and Dyvinycell™. The only organic material used is end-grain balsa wood. Because foam can degrade when heated by the sun, many manufacturers use foam in the hull and balsa in the deck, with plywood in highly loaded areas.

In areas where through-hull fittings, sharp corners, and hull-to-deck joints are placed, the core is usually eliminated entirely. You can easily find out from the builder of your boat how the hull was built. If it is cored and you want to add extra through-hull fittings or make other holes in the hull, you should ask the manufacturer if there are any areas that may be drilled without having to strip the core out and refair the laminate.

THE HULL PLUG AND MOLD

When a boat is first put into production, a plug and a mold must be made. Accepted practice is to make a complete wooden plug that looks just like the finished hull of the boat. It may have a stub for the keel and a flat for the rudder, but in all other respects it will look like the hull of the first yacht of that series.

Over that a mold is laid up. Like a mold for casting a statue, the hull mold fits exactly over the outside of the boat. All future boats will be laid up in this mold, which is strongly reinforced and highly polished.

To make the plug, the lines plan of the yacht is lofted accurately and totally faired. Then the planking thickness is deducted from the lofted lines on each section. These sections are cut out; often you'll see them stacked to one side ready for use. Next a strongback is made. This will carry the entire weight of the hull plug. Usually the strongback is fabricated out of 2-inch by 10- or 12-inch (50 mm

15

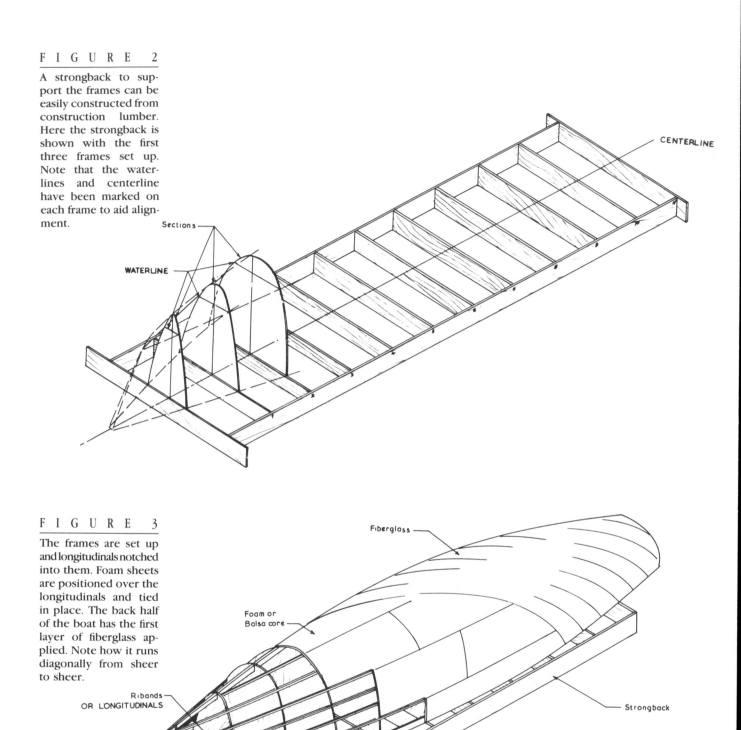

F I G U R E   2

A strongback to support the frames can be easily constructed from construction lumber. Here the strongback is shown with the first three frames set up. Note that the waterlines and centerline have been marked on each frame to aid alignment.

CENTERLINE

Sections

WATERLINE

F I G U R E   3

The frames are set up and longitudinals notched into them. Foam sheets are positioned over the longitudinals and tied in place. The back half of the boat has the first layer of fiberglass applied. Note how it runs diagonally from sheer to sheer.

Fiberglass

Foam or Balsa core

Strongback

Ribands OR LONGITUDINALS

Sheer

× 250 mm or 300 mm) planking. A sketch of a strong-back is shown in Figure 2. Next the sections are set up, upside down, on the strongback and fastened into place. Here the plug-building technique can vary.

If the boat is to be a limited production run or a one-off, some builders fasten ribands to the sections and cover them with foam. The foam is temporarily glued or sewn into place to provide a smooth layer for the fiberglass laminates. These laminates form the outer skin of the hull. This method of building is shown in Figure 3. When the fiberglass work has set up solidly, the hull is faired and undercoated. Then a cradle is made to fit the hull precisely, and the entire unit turned over. The sections and ribands are stripped out, leaving a bare foam interior. Fiberglass is laid up over this interior until the required hull thickness has been achieved. At this stage the hull is rigid and ready for the interior furniture. (This is discussed in more detail later in this chapter.)

For a series production mold, a builder will usually make a wooden hull plug, using strips of wood or even plywood sheets to fabricate the shape of the hull plug. In fact, after it is painted and polished, ready for laying up the mold, the plug is almost indistinguishable from the finished hull.

After the sections are set up, they are covered with closely spaced ribands of 1-inch by 1-inch (25 mm × 25 mm) pine. Some builders add extra layers of ⅛- or ¹⁄₁₀-inch (3 mm or 2.5 mm) strip planking, laid diagonally across the hull while other builders go straight to the next step. That is, the laying up of two or three layers of fiberglass cloth. The cloth is glued tightly to the plug and the entire unit faired up carefully. After polishing and waxing—using mold release wax—the plug is ready to receive the mold.

The mold is laid up over the plug. (Fiberglass, when wetted out with polyester resin, assumes the shape of the object it is draped over; however, polyester or vinylester resins are thermosetting resins, and once the laminate has dried, the fiberglass and resin are permanently fixed in that shape.) Usually molds are built with massive reinforcement. Steel tubes and heavy-duty plywood are all used to maintain the shape of the mold. A typical mold

may be used to produce up to one hundred boats, so distortion is totally undesirable. As each boat is laid up in the mold, a little heat is given off from the curing fiberglass; this heat tends to reduce the life of the mold, necessitating a very heavy mold laminate and plenty of reinforcement.

INTERIOR LINERS

Sometimes called an interior pan, this piece of fiberglass has several functions. It often gives structural rigidity to the hull, supports the furniture, and provides foundations for machinery and equipment. It fits inside the hull, replacing frames and longitudinals, and is firmly glassed and epoxied in place.

The pan is made the same way as the hull is made, in that it is laminated from fiberglass cloth and mat. Large, flat areas are usually reinforced with balsa or foam core, making the whole structure fairly rigid.

A typical full pan will cover the entire hull interior from sheer to sheer. It may have a spider set under it to carry the loads of the keel and rig. It will have the V-berth bunk faces and flats, a shower pan, locker ceiling, settee berth faces and flats on both sides of the interior, support for the nav table, support for the galley, quarter berth flats and faces, and usually the engine sump pan and bearers. Figure 4 shows a pan, spider, and hull. Note the plywood bulkheads and bunk access holes and covers. Compare that with the boat shown in Figure 5, where all the components are fitted separately. The number of parts in the structural part of the boat is dramatically reduced.

Some builders only use a half pan. This is a liner that covers the bilge area and has structural frames and floors built into it. The remainder of the interior is then fabricated from wood, giving the boat a more traditional appearance.

Other builders use a pan only in the toilet compartment on larger boats. In this position it serves as a shower pan and support for the toilet. Often a sump tank is combined with this unit, making plumbing quite simple.

For retrofitting or rebuilding the interior of your boat, the smaller the pan is, the easier the job will be. In general

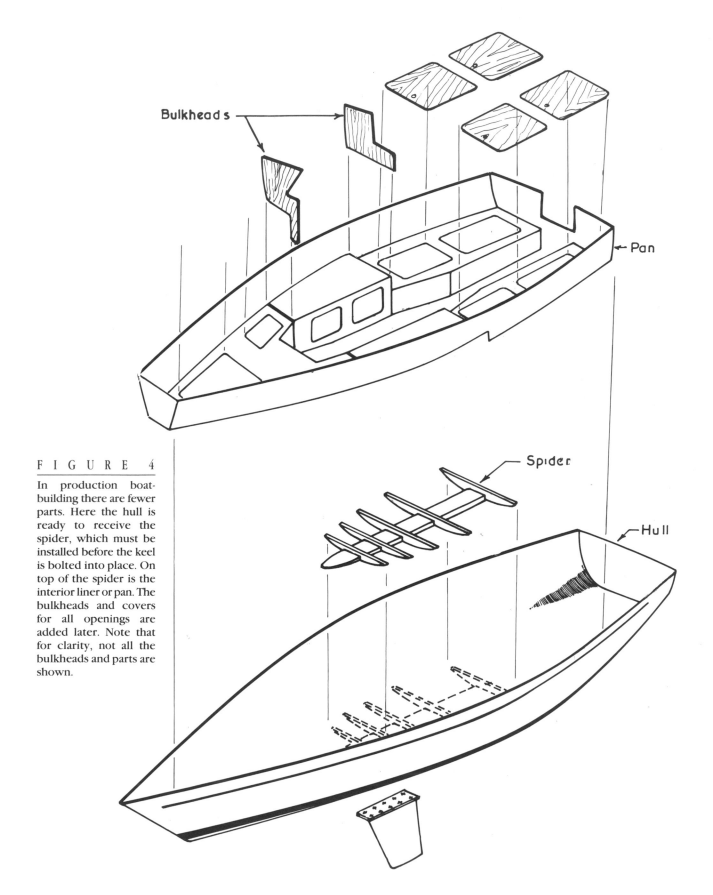

Bulkheads

Pan

Spider

Hull

F I G U R E 4

In production boat-building there are fewer parts. Here the hull is ready to receive the spider, which must be installed before the keel is bolted into place. On top of the spider is the interior liner or pan. The bulkheads and covers for all openings are added later. Note that for clarity, not all the bulkheads and parts are shown.

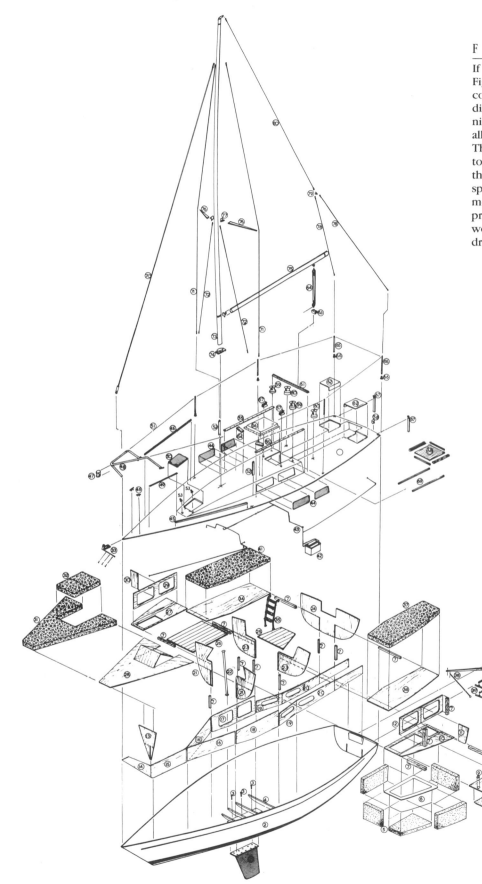

F I G U R E   5

If the boat shown in Figure 4 were to be constructed using traditional fitting-out techniques, it would have all the parts shown here. Think how long it takes to cut and fit each of these parts. More time spent fitting out would mean that the cost of producing the boat would be increased dramatically.

a large pan firmly fixed to the hull has been designed to be part of the structural strength of the boat. Cutting extensive portions away could lead to serious rigidity problems and possibly render the entire craft inoperable. So, consult your builder *before* making any drastic cuts.

FURNITURE

It used to be, and still is in custom yards, that a man would go aboard a boat, measure where a piece of furniture was to be fitted, and build that piece inside the boat. This is the way the vessel illustrated in Figure 5 would have to be built. Today only the most expensive boat builders do that. Most manufacturers build the furniture outside the boat and install it directly onto foundations provided by the interior liner. The furniture is installed before the deck is fitted, often making it impossible to remove without totally destroying the unit.

On the modern production boat, then, very little is built inside the boat. More work done outside the boat makes for a more consistent quality at a lower price. It also means time saved by the craftsman, who would have to step on and off the boat eight or ten times to measure and fit one piece of joinery.

BULKHEADS

These large pieces of plywood are also cut to size and installed before the deck is fitted. They are jigged up in the furniture shop, and often several are cut at once. At the boat they are dropped into slots in the interior pan, bedded in compound, and bolted into place, the whole job taking a few minutes.

THE DECK AND DECK LINER

Like the hull, the deck is laid up in a female mold. It is then trimmed and set up, ready to receive deck fittings. While it is being readied, the deck liner is popped out of its mold and prepped. The deck and liner may be com-

bined at any stage, depending on the manufacturer. Usually some deck fittings are bolted to the deck, while the wiring harness is installed in the liner. Then the two are combined by epoxying and glassing together.

At this point the deck is not yet bolted to the hull. All the deck fittings except the toerail are bolted into place. This includes hatches, winches, cleats, steering pedestals, and mast fittings. Under the deck the lights are wired up together with any vents or interior trim around the hatches and ports. Then the deck is ready to be bolted to the hull.

FITTING THE ENGINE

In most of the larger manufacturing plants the interior pan has the engine bearers already molded in. Quite often the engine bolts are in place. The boat manufacturer simply drops the engine into the pan and bolts it down. Wiring and plumbing for the engine have already been built in, and all the installer has to do is connect everything up. With the engine and all the interior furniture installed, the deck is ready to be added.

FITTING THE DECK

There are many variations in hull-deck joints. Some are stronger than others, and some cannot stand up to the strain of holding the boat together. The most popular styles are shown in Figures 6 through 10.

Figure 6 is usually only seen on custom craft. Here the hull is built with an outward-turning flange, making it easy to build, and the deck is built slightly larger than needed. The two pieces are laid on top of each other and bolted together (shown dashed). This ensures accurate alignment. Once the flange is thoroughly bolted, the joint can be glassed on the inside with several layers of fiberglass. The flange is then cut off and the exterior glass laminates applied. When enough glass has been applied, the exterior of the joint is cleaned up and faired, ready to be painted. As you can see, this type of joint entails a fair amount of work.

There are many variations on this joint. One is to screw

20

a piece of wood around the interior face of the hull and then screw the deck to the wood. The wooden flange is then totally encapsulated with the layers of fiberglass. This adds stiffness and rigidity to the joint.

A simpler joint is the one shown in Figure 7. Sometimes called a coffee-can joint, this one has a downward-turning flange on the deck that fits over the hull. The joint is then glassed, through-bolted, and the rubrail bolted on—a quick, simple, and effective joint. It is cleaner when the deck has a slight recess, as shown, but most often it is done as shown in Figure 7A, where the deck is simply trimmed and bolted.

The height of the joint can vary. For instance, if the designer wants to put a rubrail around the hull, he may hide the joint behind the rubrail. With careful design, this can disguise a high freeboard. If the edge of the hull-deck intersection does look too high, one method of making it look lower is to slope the edge of the deck inboard slightly and set the hull-deck joint about 10 or 12 inches lower than the sheerline. When the sloping part of the deck is painted a contrasting color, the hull can be made to look reasonably attractive.

Figures 8 and 8A show variations on bolting vertically. In Figure 8 the deck is set into a recess in the hull flange and bolted. Usually a toerail is used to cover the joint and give it extra rigidity. This type of joint is often seen around the transom of many production yachts when it is simply filled and leveled. In Figure 8A the deck runs to the edge of the hull, where it is covered with an aluminum toerail. In this case the rail provides stiffness and strength.

The joints in Figures 9 and 9A are not often seen on sailing craft, as they have a slight problem. There have been instances where the outward-turning flange has caught under or on a dock or piling and damaged the joint. However, if you can keep away from docks and pilings, they are quite strong.

Figure 10 shows a joint where the flange has been turned into a bulwark. This is quite a strong way of making the joint, but waterways need to be cut through the bulwark to allow drainage. Often it is at the waterway that leakage will occur. If you have this type of hull-deck joint and have a leak below deck, the first place you should

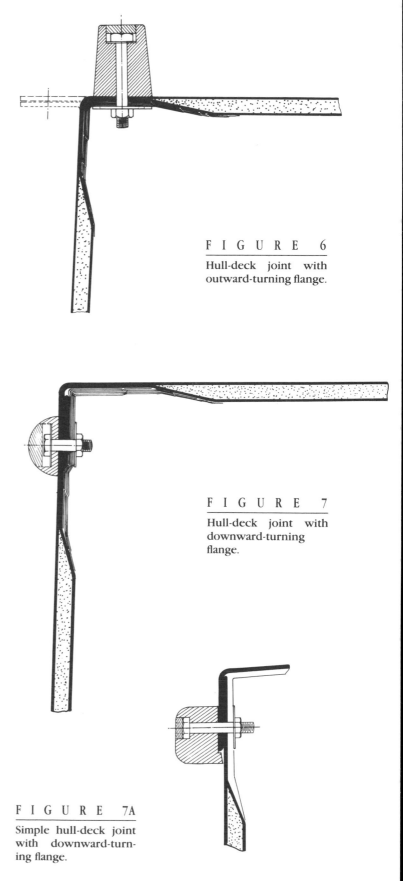

FIGURE 6

Hull-deck joint with outward-turning flange.

FIGURE 7

Hull-deck joint with downward-turning flange.

FIGURE 7A

Simple hull-deck joint with downward-turning flange.

look for the source of the leak should be where waterways have been cut through the bulwark.

These are a few of the stronger hull-deck joints and some of their drawbacks. Given the impermeability of fiberglass decks, any leak is likely to start at the hull-deck joint, and a strong, well-sealed joint is an essential part of any boat.

Having seen how a production boat is put together, we must now look at the changes that can easily be made without compromising the structural integrity of the vessel. These changes can be many, from adding a small port or hatch, to adding a bedside table or extra counter space in the galley. In the following pages we'll look at the changes that can easily be made to a production boat.

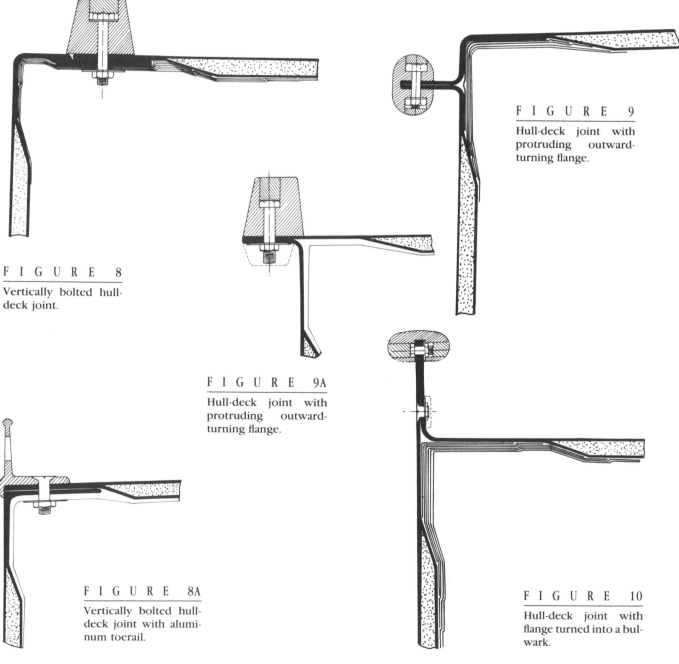

FIGURE 9
Hull-deck joint with protruding outward-turning flange.

FIGURE 8
Vertically bolted hull-deck joint.

FIGURE 9A
Hull-deck joint with protruding outward-turning flange.

FIGURE 8A
Vertically bolted hull-deck joint with aluminum toerail.

FIGURE 10
Hull-deck joint with flange turned into a bulwark.

CUSTOM AND SEMI-CUSTOM YACHT CONSTRUCTION

Custom yacht construction differs from production building in the methods of building the boat. As we saw, a production yacht is assembled from large, premolded pieces and prefabricated interior fittings as economically as possible. A custom yacht, on the other hand, has a hull built over a one-off mold and may have an interior built piece by piece inside the boat. Depending on the method of construction, the hull mold is usually built as inexpensively as possible and thrown away after use.

A custom yacht's hull can be of many materials. The most common are sandwich-cored fiberglass, wood (often WEST system), and metal (either alloy or steel). An amateur builder might want to build using ferroconcrete, but that material is extremely labor-intensive.

SANDWICH-CORED FIBERGLASS BOATS

If a custom yacht is to be built out of fiberglass, then the hull will probably be cored with either foam or end-grain balsa. Building a single-skin fiberglass hull for a one-off is not cost-effective.

If a builder intends to build a single-skin hull, he will need to make a complete mold before the hull can be laid up, just as the production builder must. This is because the fiberglass, when wet, does not have any strength or rigidity. It will simply conform to whatever shape it is laid over.

One method of building a cored hull that gives the builder a relatively inexpensive method of making a mold for the hull is to use frames and ribands rather than a complete hull plug. As we saw in Figures 2 and 3, the temporary frames are set up and long ribands (strips of 1-inch by 1-inch (25 mm × 25 mm)) wood are nailed to the frames about 6 to 8 inches (150 mm to 200 mm) apart. The core material is fastened to the ribands by either

gluing or sewing, and the entire exterior sanded smooth. This forms a mold for the fiberglass to be laid up on.

The outer laminate is now laid up, layer by layer. Care is taken to ensure that it is smooth and even throughout the process. When the entire skin has been laid, the outside is faired until it is smooth. To fair the hull, epoxy resin with microbaloons or other fillers are used to fill voids and hollows. Once the hull is reasonably fair, it is sanded with longboards—6-inch-wide, 2- to 3-foot-long (150 mm wide, .6 to 1 m long) boards. Sanding a high-performance boat can take weeks, but usually the entire job is completed in a few days. Quite often the hull is primed and even topcoated before it is removed from the framing.

At this stage the hull, when all the framing has been stripped out, is very rubbery, so a strong supporting cradle is assembled. Then the entire unit is rolled over—the hull is now upright for the first time. Once it is upright and well supported, the sections, longitudinals, and temporary structure are stripped out and the interior laminate laid up over the core material. Again the work must be kept as fair and clean as possible. Now the bulkheads can be positioned and glassed in place, increasing the hull rigidity even more. Usually the structural members are installed at the same time and the hull shape is firmly fixed. At this point the hull is stiff and ready for furniture and equipment.

WOODEN BOATS

Most modern wooden hulls are constructed using epoxies, of which the most well known is the WEST™ system, developed by the Gougeon brothers. Older hulls are constructed using more traditional methods. Here we will look at both methods.

Wooden boat building in the traditional manner has largely died out in the United States. However, there are a number of yards overseas that still use wood in the old style. This section is also for the reader who wants to make changes in a traditionally built wooden boat.

The wood used was usually only obtainable in reasonably short lengths, consequently a skilled builder had to make a homogeneous boat out of short pieces of wood. This put a premium on joints and distributing the loads in the right direction. Consequently wooden-boat-building methods were not precalculated. They evolved as the craftsman became more practiced in his art. Some organizations attempted to introduce scantlings to enable builders to obtain consistent results. The scantling rules developed by Lloyd's Register of Shipping were the most well used in Britain, while Herreshoff's rules and Nevin's scantling rules were the most well-known wood structural scantlings used in America. Many designers still use these scantlings today to develop the structure of wooden boats.

Figure 11 shows the parts of a wooden boat. Note how the frames are spaced at regular intervals down the length of the boat and the diagonal strapping for additional longitudinal stiffness. In Britain, boats would be built using a bilge stringer rather than the diagonal strapping. If you intend to modify a wooden boat, it is best to leave these structural parts alone unless you have skilled knowledge of the effects of the changes.

Bulkheads are another part of the boat that may be structural or nonstructural, and a simple cutout can affect the entire vessel. For instance, two identical sister ships were built at a well-known yard in Britain, except that one had a cutout in the main bulkhead, just aft of the mast, to fit a diesel cabin heater. The cutout was about 30×14 inches (760 mm $\times$ 355 mm). Both boats were in severe storm conditions of about force eight gusting nine. When they reached harbor, the boat with the heater had fractured the bulkhead cleanly across in way of the

F I G U R E   11

The construction of a traditionally built boat.

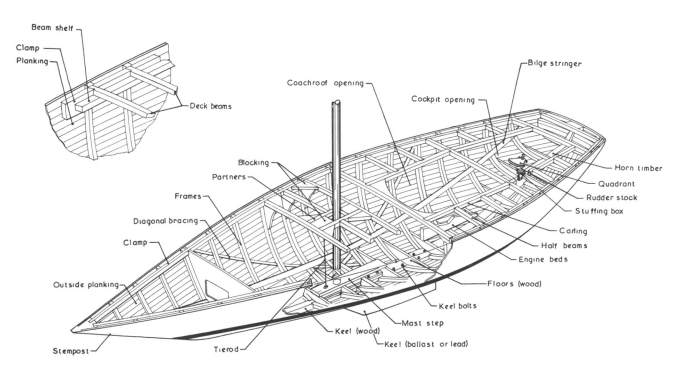

24

cutout. It was a simple, seemingly innocuous opening, but it had weakened the bulkhead sufficiently for the fracture to take place.

Boats built using the WEST system are built in a very different way. The Wood Epoxy Saturation Technique (WEST™) is supposed to encapsulate each piece of wood in an epoxy that binds it to its neighbor. This produces a hull that can be thought of as a monocoque structure with evenly distributed loads. Consequently the scantlings may be much lighter than a similar traditionally constructed wooden boat. In fact, some boats have been built with scantlings up to 50 percent lighter. Obviously this places even more of a premium on structural fittings and bulkheads.

To build a WEST™-system yacht, a plug must be made. This is built in a fashion similar to the one used for one-off sandwich-cored hulls, in that sections are set up and ribands set into those sections to provide a rigid plug. Some builders like to reduce material costs and build the backbone, frames, and floors directly into the plug so that they become part of the boat as it is built. Sometimes just the bulkheads are installed later, after the hull is turned over and the plug stripped out. When the plug is finished, long strips of veneer are laid over it and stapled lightly to it. The first layer of strips are edge-glued. Later layers are glued to the previous layer and each other.

Depending on the finish required, the veneers may be laid diagonally or longitudinally along the hull. Usually the hull is made laying the strips diagonally across the hull and a horizontal layer added if the exterior is to be finished with a clear varnish. If a clear finished inside is required, horizontal strips are laid in after the hull is turned over and the temporary frames stripped out.

When the hull is right side up, the remainder of the interior structure is built in. Then the deck is added and the structure becomes a rigid unit.

METAL BOATS

Metal boats are vessels built either from steel or aluminum. While steel is often considered the ideal metal for an amateur builder, it has several drawbacks. One is its low corrosion resistance. Steel boats have to be maintained on an almost continual basis. The problem is a lot less severe than it was many years ago; however, with today's epoxy paints, the hull should keep its shine for several years if dings and scratches are touched up promptly.

It is inside a steel boat that corrosion can be more of a problem. If the frames and longitudinals are not designed to allow water drainage, water can rest in one place and cause rust. Quite often this rust will be behind a piece of furniture, where it is not seen until it is almost too late. For this reason it is better to build a steel boat with the minimum number of frames and longitudinals and to cut drain holes where possible.

This does, however, pose a problem for the person who wants to add extra lockers or change the interior layout. There may not be anything to attach the woodwork to inside the boat. To get around this problem, flat lugs or brackets may have to be welded to the hull. Any new furniture can then be bolted to these brackets.

When welding is performed inside the boat, the exterior must be repainted because the heat of welding will burn off any paint. You should also check the outside of the hull or deck to ensure that your new weld will not burn anything important, such as a wooden rubrail, a winch base, or the deck covering. If it does, you might have to replace the entire unit.

Aluminum yachts are a different proposition. In general they are made with reasonably thin plating and many frames and longitudinals, which gives a wide range of places to attach new furniture. If you are adding an item of gear, you may want to make an aluminum foundation using angle brackets. This can be fabricated outside the boat and easily bolted or welded into place. Beware, though, of drilling too many closely spaced holes in high-stress areas. It could cause the part to fail.

Both aluminum and steel boats may suffer greatly from electrolysis or galvanic corrosion. This occurs when stray electrical current combines with seawater to turn the boat into a giant battery. If this occurs, a through-hull fitting or a sacrificial anode could corrode within a matter of hours. Then the corrosion starts eating into your boat!

For this reason, it pays to be extra careful when adding new wiring or other electrical items to a metal boat.

Boats, then, are not built exactly the same way. You will have to understand a little about how your boat is put together in order to take it apart. Obviously you do not want to ruin your yacht; it represents a significant investment. If you have any doubt about your ability to retrofit any fitting or modify any existing item, seek qualified advice before embarking on the project. Advice is cheap, experience is a lot more expensive!

TOOLS AND USEFUL EQUIPMENT

Many of the projects illustrated here require a range of tools and equipment. Some of them will be used only once—in that case, if they are expensive, you may want to rent them. Inexpensive tools, such as fiberglass rollers or resin spreaders, should be thrown out after a few uses. Don't make the mistake of scrimping on tools and hoping you'll do a good job. The best workmen may get away with doing that, but amateurs usually can't. Tools can be divided into several categories: tools for glasswork, for woodwork, for metalwork, and power tools. Many tools, such as saws, drills, sanders, and so on, can be used for working with almost any material. Here they are listed as commonly used tools, with tools specific to the material discussed under that material.

COMMONLY USED TOOLS FOR ALL MATERIALS

Most people have basic tools and are familiar with their usage. By that I mean such tools as a hammer, handsaw, drill and drill bits, tape measure, and clamps. However, for the novice here's a brief rundown on them.

HAMMERS

If the truth be told, a hammer has no place on a boat. It should not be used for driving screws or fitting a recalcitrant bolt. Its only use is for nailing together temporary structures, such as a simple scaffold to help you work on the outside of the boat, and even then the scaffolding will be safer and stronger if the pieces are screwed together. The only other place I've seen a hammer used is to nail the strongback and frames together when constructing the mold for the dinghy shown in Chapter 7. If you need a hammer for this, it should be a woodworker's claw-type weighing about a pound (0.45 kg).

Metalworking hammers are an entirely different tool. In this case a ball peen hammer should be used. Ideally you should have several, weighing from a few ounces to

3 pounds (a few grams to 2.5 kg). They are used for turning over rivet heads, hammering hollows or curves into metal, and bending short pieces of metal.

HANDSAWS

Mostly for woodworking, handsaws are an indispensable tool for quick, short cuts. You should have a good-quality tenon saw, a good crosscut saw, and a ripsaw for woodworking. A top-quality tenon saw should have a heavy brass back to give it plenty of rigidity. If you intend to use it solely for finish work, it should have a high ratio of teeth per inch. Crosscut saws, as their name implies, are used for cutting across the grain of the wood without ripping it. They are usually reasonably fine (many teeth per inch), which eliminates splintered ends on the wood. A ripsaw is used for cutting with the grain. Usually they cut fast and coarsely. The assumption here is that the side of the wood will be planed up smoothly.

For cutting metal a hacksaw is best. Various different blades can be purchased. The finer the blade (more teeth per inch), the slower and cleaner the cut is. Use fine blades on thin materials and coarser blades on thicker metals. Hacksaws can be used on fiberglass, but because of their design they can only make relatively short cuts.

POWER SAWS

For rough work cutting straight sections on long pieces of wood, a hand-held circular saw will give a reasonably accurate cut if it is used carefully. Ideally a table saw is best, but not many amateurs have access to them.

For cutting large diameter circles in wood, thin metal, or fiberglass, a saber saw or jigsaw is best. Ideally you should select one that is powerful enough to plunge into a piece of wood and start cutting. These are the top of the line and are usually quite expensive. Lower down the scale is the type that will cut wood or metal provided they start at the edge or in a predrilled hole.

DRILLS AND DRILL BITS

Today most workers use electric drills. Ideally a reversing, variable-speed drill is best, but it's expensive. Select one with the largest chuck capacity you can afford; most go to ½ inch (12 mm). If you can afford it or can get access to a drill press, this will give you more accurate holes than a hand-held drill.

Some workers prefer a cordless saw to get to those inaccessible areas where power cables could get snagged. If you decide to use a cordless saw, make sure you have a spare battery pack handy to prevent having to stop halfway through the job when the battery dies.

You should have a variety of drill bits—high-speed woodworking bits and lower-speed metalworking bits. A general rule of thumb is to use a lower drill speed for larger diameter bits, so a variable-speed drill is useful if you intend to drill different diameter holes.

SCREWDRIVERS

A selection of screwdrivers is always useful. Make sure you have ones small enough to drive the smallest screw you intend using. Nothing looks worse than to see the area around a woodscrew chewed up because too large a screwdriver was used. Flat-bladed screwdrivers are best for slotted screws, but Phillips-head screws and other variations are becoming much more common. In America the most common screwhead is the Phillips because it can be driven with an electric drill using a special bit. This saves time and gives a cleaner, more symmetrical look to the job. If you decide to use a slotted screw, you can get a better, more professional look to the job if all the slots are lined up in the direction of the wood grain.

TAPE MEASURES

Ideally you will need two or three tape measures. One to lose, one about 6 feet (2 m) long, and another about 25 or 30 feet (7.5 m or 10 m) long. If you are doing mast work, you'll need a 100-foot (30-m) tape. They should be fiberglass or metal; cloth ones tend to stretch over time.

SQUARES

Nothing in a yacht is square, so why use one, I was asked a few years ago. Unfortunately, my questioner was partly right, but furniture and bulkheads must be square, so you will need one. Preferably find one about 24 or 30 inches (.6 m or .76 m) on a side. A shorter one is often handy for tight locations.

LEVELS

If the boat is set up level, installing new furniture is made much easier if a level is used. A small one, sometimes called a torpedo level, is ideal for tight spots, but one about 24 inches (.6 m) or longer is useful to ensure that bulkheads or other large pieces of joinerwork are perfectly vertical.

CLAMPS

A good builder will have a selection of clamps. There should be C- or G-clamps, pipe clamps, and even rubber band clamps. If possible, you should have three or four of each type as a minimum. They should be sized correctly for the job rather than having to clamp a small item with a giant clamp.

CAULKING GUNS

Of all the tools used on a boat, none has a greater effect than a caulking gun. Every piece of deck gear that is bolted through the deck should be caulked to seal out seawater. I once raced on a boat on which the owner had repositioned most of the deck gear. He hadn't used any caulking, and when it rained—which it did just as we were about to turn it—the interior of the boat turned into a shower. We had to wear foul-weather gear below deck to stay dry! When purchasing a caulking gun, buy two. You will usually get one so messy that the only solution will be to throw it away.

BENCH VISES

All good workers will have some method of holding the job in place while it is worked on. In most cases a bench vise is the best item. Woodworkers often have them built into the workbench, while metalwork vises are much more substantial and should be solidly bolted to the bench top. It is also useful to have a smaller, movable vise for moving the job from the bench to, say, the drill press.

TOOLS FOR WORKING WITH FIBERGLASS

The resins used with fiberglass can be dangerous to your health. Therefore you should make sure you have plenty of disposable gloves, overalls, and rags handy. Having said that, you will need some spreaders, rollers, funnels, and trays. Most of them can be purchased reasonably cheaply, but the spreaders and rollers are specific to glasswork. Chopper guns, compressors, and the like are expensive and should only be purchased if you intend to do a lot of glasswork. If so, you are probably beyond the range of this book.

SPREADERS

Spreaders are used to spread the resin after it has been applied to the fiberglass. They are simply large, flat metal or plastic boards used to push the liquid resin around.

SHEARS OR KNIVES AND STRAIGHTEDGES

These are used for cutting fiberglass. They should be as large as possible and very sharp. If you intend cutting Kevlar™ or carbon fiber, you may need heavy-duty shears.

ROLLERS

Rollers are used to roll the resin into the fiberglass. Once the resin has been laid over the glass, it has to be rolled to ensure that it penetrates the laminate and in order to remove air bubbles. Over-rolling is almost as bad as under-rolling. Under-rolling can result in missed areas or poor penetration, which reduces the tensile strength of the laminate; over-rolling, on the other hand, can also reduce the tensile strength of the laminate. If you want to learn to roll the resin out properly, you should make up a laminate on a sheet of glass. As you roll, look at the underside of the glass and note the progress of the air bubbles. Going back and forth about six or seven times should be plenty.

WOODWORKING TOOLS

There is something very satisfying about working with wood. It's nonpolluting, warm in winter, cool in summer, reasonably easy to work, and, when finished properly, can be beautiful. I believe wood should be worked by hand. Most of the projects shown in these pages are made of wood, and almost all require a fair amount of hand work. Tools for woodworking should be sharp: Paring a piece of wood with a sharp chisel is wonderfully satisfying; but if the chisel is blunt, the job becomes a chore. There is a vast variety of woodworking tools—several books could be devoted to describing their use, maintenance, and history. Here we'll look at the most common tools for working on today's boat and ignore tools such as the adze, which was a common boat-building tool of yesteryear.

PLANES

There is something truly pleasant about planing a nice piece of wood. The sing of the plane, its harmony with the wood, the rhythmic movement, all combine to produce one of this busy world's better moments. Unfortunately most people prefer not to use a hand plane, but rely on electric planers and high-powered routers to shape wood accurately. I like hand planes, from the huge jack planes to the smallest finger planes. A good woodworker will have a selection of planes and know how to sharpen and use them.

The jack plane is best for long, straight pieces of wood. It needs constant attention to get a level, true surface, but the satisfaction is worth it. However, a machined flat surface can be obtained faster and with more accuracy by using a small bench planer.

Jointing planes and other small sizes are best for shorter lengths of wood. Remember to plane with the grain, not against it, for best results. The tiniest planes of all are the finger planes—so called because they are held with two fingers. They are used for small detail work.

CHISELS

A good set of sharp chisels is worth its weight in gold. There are several types: firmer chisels, used entirely by hand and never hammered; mortise chisels, which come with a metal ring around the top of the handle, and are used for cutting mortises and are hammered with a wooden mallet. Then there are the plastic-handled cheapo chisels sold at supermarkets. In my opinion these are worthless. They don't hold an edge for long, and the metal quality is usually very poor. Get the best set of chisels you can afford. Keep them very sharp and protect them from your associates, who will want to borrow them and will probably ruin them.

MITER BOX

A miter box is handy for cutting accurate corners for mirrors, doors, and some hatch frames. It should have 45-degree and 90-degree slots for accurate cuts. While this is not an essential, it will definitely improve the quality of your work.

METALWORKING TOOLS

The tools required for metalworking are usually much more substantial than those used for wood or glass work. For instance, a hacksaw with changeable blades is best for cutting metal bar. When the blade wears out, you can throw it away or make another tool with it and insert a new one. Metalworking tools also depend upon the type of metalworking you may be doing. For instance, a sheet metal worker installing a metal liner in an icebox will require heavy-duty shears and metal-bending tools. A worker who machines solid metal blocks to make clamps or rudder stocks will require a lathe or milling machine.

SHEARS

These can be the same as those used for glasswork if they are a heavy-duty type. Shears are mostly used for cutting sheet metal.

WRENCHES

Wrenches are called spanners in Great Britain. The top-notch craftsperson will have a complete set of wrenches to fit all the nuts and bolts he or she is likely to use. Unfortunately, such a set is expensive, and parts easily get lost. A carefully selected set of adjustable wrenches comes a close second. They cost less and are much more versatile. However, incorrect adjustment often results in skinned knuckles. Ideally you should have a selection of open-ended types, ring- or closed-ended types, and a few box- or plug-type wrenches.

Try to purchase a kit that will not rust if it is kept aboard the boat. There are some (very expensive) kits on the market that are made of a nonferrous alloy. They come packaged in a box that will float if it's dropped over the side. Having never having used these tools, I hesitate to recommend them.

FEELER GAUGES

These are a small but almost essential item to the serious metalworker. They enable you to measure the exact gap between two pieces of metal in increments of thousandths of an inch.

FILES

Most serious metalworkers will have a selection of files handy. They will range from large bastard files for rough work to very fine needle files for small detail jobs. For cleaning files you should have a wire brush (known in England as a file card). Brushing across the teeth of the file will remove many filings and prolong the life of the tool.

MICROMETER

If you intend to make accurate metal fittings, then a micrometer is an essential tool. It measures in thousandths of an inch or millimeters and is used to measure the width or diameter of metalwork accurately.

POWER TOOLS

Power tools are expensive, but if you can get access to them, they will cut the time down by a huge amount. The most commonly used power tool is probably the electric drill, which we mentioned earlier. Other power tools you may decide are essential will usually be determined by the type of material you may be working on. For instance, a power planer may be useful for woodworking, but a disk grinder or heavy-duty sander may be best for glasswork. A metalworker might prefer a grinding wheel rather than an abrasive disk.

HAND-HELD POWER PLANER

This is useful for narrow strips of wood where a lot of material has to be removed in a short time. Power planers are used most often in boatyards to remove lead from keels that need to be reshaped. At this job they excel.

BENCH-TOP PLANER

For reducing the thickness of boards to suit the job at hand, these planers are ideal. Cut, speed, and thickness of board can usually be adjusted easily, giving a board exactly the right size in one or two passes.

DRILL PRESS

For accurate holes a drill press is essential. Usually speed of rotation and depth and position of the hole can be adjusted with great accuracy.

LATHE

Where any tubular or circular work is involved, a lathe is essential. Woodworking lathes are usually less expensive than metalworking lathes. Ideally the woodworking lathe should have variable speed of rotation, high torque, adjustable chuck and tail stock, and be easy to operate.

Metalworking lathes will have additional features, such as screw-cutting feed, changeable tool holder, a hollow chuck to enable long pieces of metal to be worked, and an automatic tool feed.

BENCH GRINDER

For keeping tools sharp a bench grinder is an essential. It should have a rough stone on one end and a smooth stone on the other. If you can afford it, a second grinder with a grinding pad and a sanding or buffing pad will also be extremely useful.

IMPROVING YOUR DECK LAYOUT

At one time or another you have probably tried to take a line to a winch only to find that the lead was fouled. The solution was to relead the line from a less efficient angle and hope that it would work. This effort could easily have been avoided if it had been possible to fit another block. In the following pages you will see how easy it is to add an extra pad eye for a block. You will also see how winches, tracks, and stanchions are installed. An opening port, too, is also a useful addition, as is an extra track. We will also look at making gratings for the cockpit sole and see how a bow roller can be fitted. Other chapters show items that can be made for the deck. Chapter 5 covers hatches in detail, and Chapter 6 adds a dorade vent to the deck plan. In Chapter 7 we see how the addition of davits can make stowing the dinghy easier and safer.

P R O J E C T   3 - 1
MAKING A GRATING

Most gratings are built for the cockpit sole, but you might want to put a small one in the icebox or perhaps on the galley sole. In addition, a small table made from a simple grating can be a useful and eye-catching feature in the cockpit or the cabin.

To make a grating, begin with a flat piece of wood the same thickness as the finished grating (see Figure 1) and as long as the desired length of the grating. Then cut grooves in the board with either a table saw or a router. Figure 2 shows the technique. Make these grooves exactly half the depth of the original wood and the same width as the width of the grating slats that you will cut, as shown in Figure 3. The next step is to make the edge trim. This is usually about 2 to 3 inches (50 mm to 75 mm) wide and the same thickness as the grating. Use trim around every edge of the grate rather than have exposed lengths of grating visible. To attach the trim, rout a groove to hold the grating ends, as shown in Figure 4. Figure 3A shows the L-shaped groove on the underside of the finished grating, and shows how the voids left in the edge trim should be filled with precut pieces of grating. If you do not want to use small pieces of additional lumber, then cut each notch for the grating ends individually as shown in Figure 4. Dry-fit the entire grating to ensure that it goes together without jamming before gluing it in place. Do not try to force the pieces of grating together. They will split easily and ruin an otherwise good piece. Figure 5 shows the finished unit.

If you are making the grating to fit the cockpit floor and the steering column is in the way, make a cardboard or paper mock-up of the shape of the grating and use that as a template.

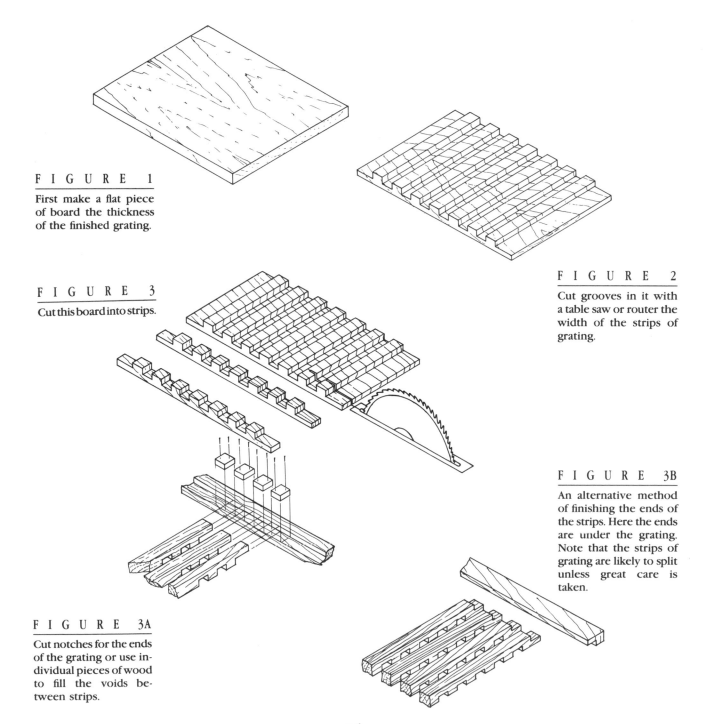

F I G U R E   1

First make a flat piece of board the thickness of the finished grating.

F I G U R E   2

Cut grooves in it with a table saw or router the width of the strips of grating.

F I G U R E   3

Cut this board into strips.

F I G U R E   3B

An alternative method of finishing the ends of the strips. Here the ends are under the grating. Note that the strips of grating are likely to split unless great care is taken.

F I G U R E   3A

Cut notches for the ends of the grating or use individual pieces of wood to fill the voids between strips.

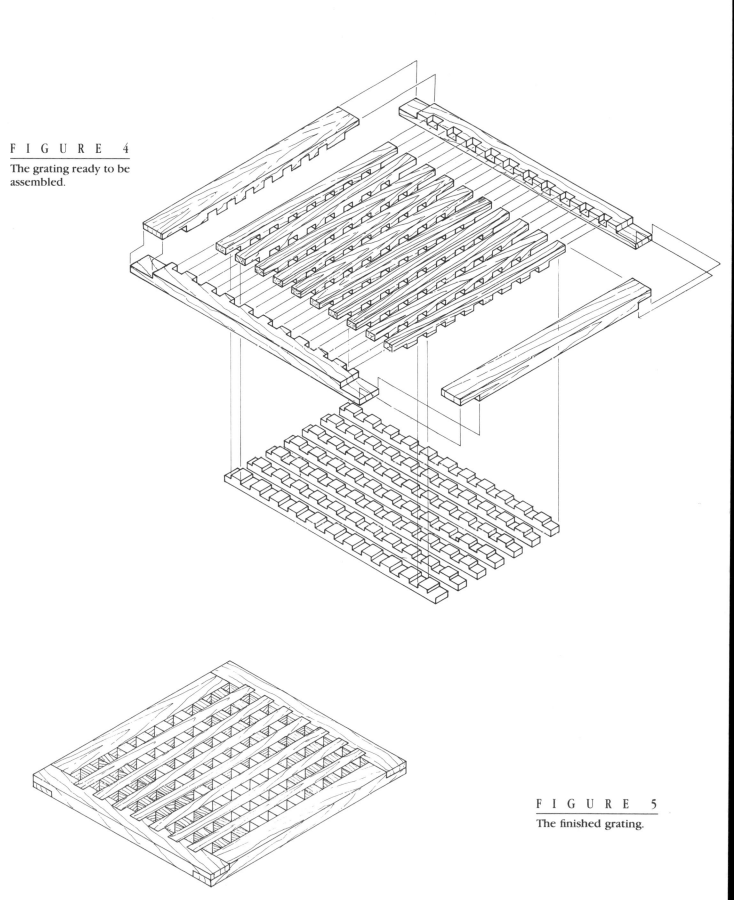

PROJECT 3 - 2

COCKPIT TABLES

In addition to a grating, a small table makes the cockpit much more livable. If you do not have the room for a table, then perhaps you could add a drink holder made out of clear plastic or an attractive wood as shown in Figure 1. It is simply a flat surface with holes drilled in it to hold glasses when the boat is at anchor or sitting in a marina. The brackets to hold it in place are made from a piece of flat, nonferrous metal (see below). Ferrous metals, such as iron or steel, can affect the compass, so do not use them. Drill and tap the pedestal to hold the brackets in place and mount the drink tray on top of them. A four-glass tray is shown in Figure 1A. You may want to modify it to hold three or six glasses, or you may decide to incorporate a small hors d'oeuvre tray and two glass holders.

Figure 2 shows a cockpit drop-leaf table. This is especially useful if you and your crew often eat in the cockpit. The table is supported by a bracket, as illustrated in Figure 4. This bracket is made of a strip of ⅛- or ¼-inch (3-mm or 6-mm) by 1- or 1 ½-inch (25-mm or 37-mm) brass or aluminum alloy. It is bent, as shown in Figure 4, and screwed to the underside of the table. The crosspiece is made of a similar strip bent to suit the pedestal. This, too, is bolted to the

pedestal by drilling and tapping the bolt holes. Note that pedestals are usually made of alloy, and an aluminum alloy strip would reduce the possibility of galvanic corrosion. Edson Corp. of New Bedford, Mass., make most steering pedestals, and it would probably be smart to consult their catalog before drilling the pedestal to ensure you do not damage some equipment inside it. Note that this bracket can be removed by lifting it out of the slot.

By making the leg foldable (illustrated in Figure 5) the entire table becomes collapsible and can be stored belowdecks when not in use. This table does, however, have a few restrictions. First, make sure the cockpit is wide enough to accommodate a drop-leaf table by making a cardboard template. If the folding leaves hit the cockpit seats, then you may want to rethink your strategy and use the table shown in Figure 3. Bear in mind that the cockpit table need not be fixed to the pedestal. It can be hinged off the bulkhead at the forward end of the cockpit.

The section on tables in Chapter 4 will give you more tips on building tables and could be helpful if you decide to make the folding cockpit table shown here. Chapter 4 also gives details on making a bulkhead-mounted table.

FIGURE 1A

The layout and dimensions of a four-glass drinks tray.

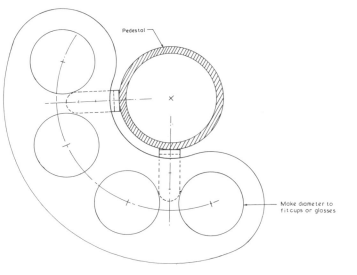

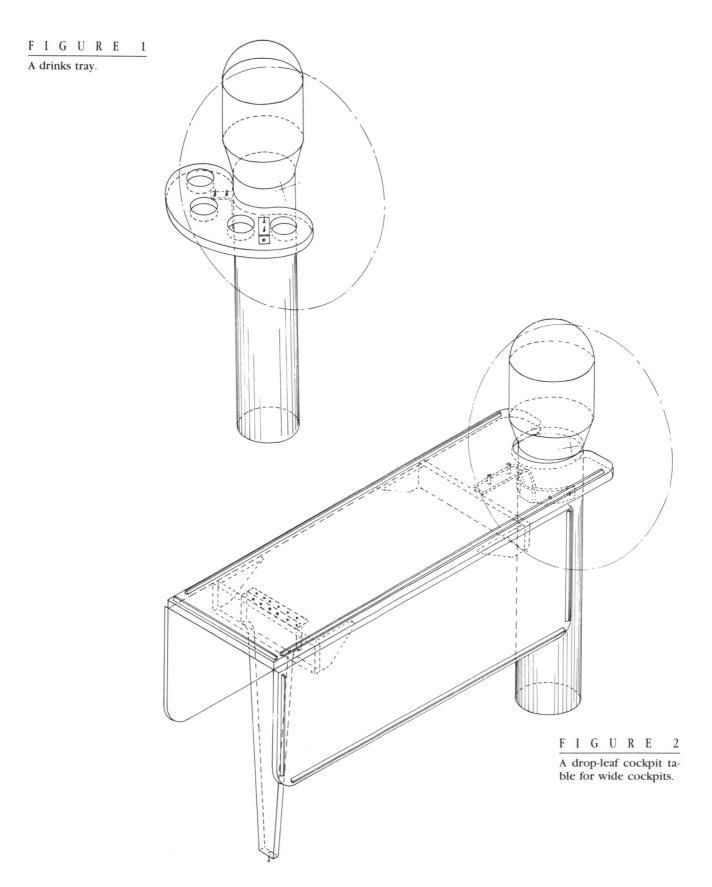

F I G U R E   2

A drop-leaf cockpit ta-
ble for wide cockpits.

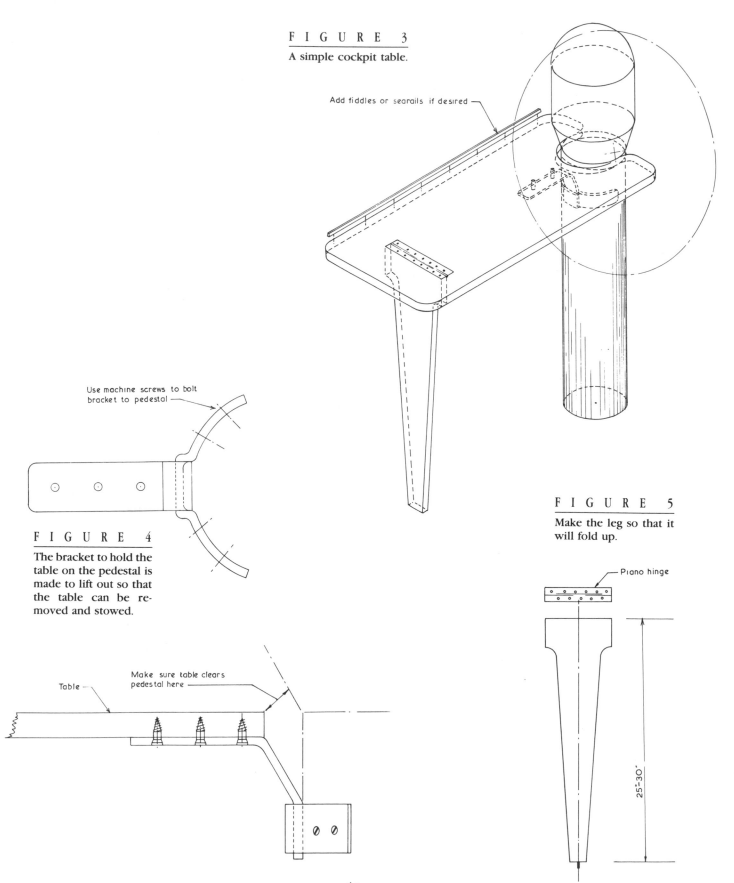

FIGURE 3
A simple cockpit table.

Add fiddles or searails if desired

Use machine screws to bolt
bracket to pedestal

FIGURE 4
The bracket to hold the
table on the pedestal is
made to lift out so that
the table can be re-
moved and stowed.

FIGURE 5
Make the leg so that it
will fold up.

Piano hinge

25"-30"

Make sure table clears
pedestal here

Table

40

PROJECT 3 - 3
ADDING NEW TRACK

Many manufacturers put the minimum amount of track on their boats and provide extra tracks as an expensive option. But a track can be bought from most marine hardware suppliers in a variety of lengths and sizes. I prefer to use either Harken or Nicro Fico tracks, but almost all of them use the same method of installation. Installing an additional track is a reasonably simple job. Figure 1 shows the procedure. First lay the track in the desired position on deck and mark the hole at either end. Check below deck, removing the overhead liner first, to make sure you are not about to drill through wiring or structural supports. Also make sure you are drilling in a reinforced portion of the deck. (If it is not, see the methods of reinforcing the deck below.) Now

drill a hole at either end of the track. Bolt the track to its backing plate through the holes you have just drilled. Next mark the remaining holes. (The track manufacturers do not like you to drill through the track to position the holes, but most people do it anyway.) With the holes marked, you should remove the track and drill the remaining holes. It is now a simple job to put a friend belowdecks to hold the nuts while you screw down the track. Remember to caulk the back of the track before it is bolted down. If you do not, you may get a leak or two belowdecks. Once the track is bolted down, you can reinstall the overhead liner, and the job is done.

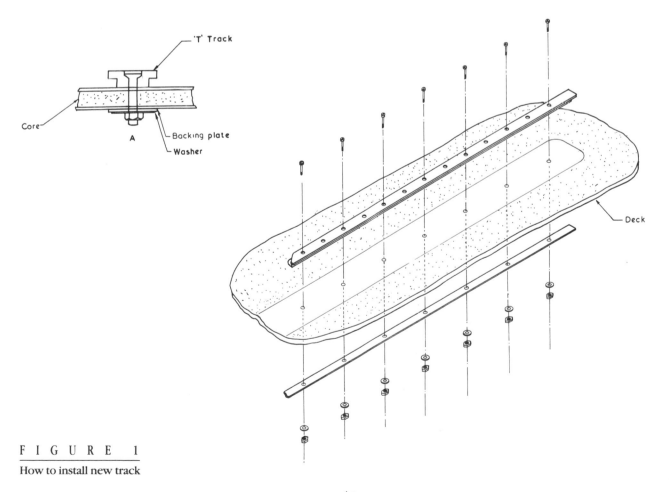

FIGURE 1

How to install new track

ADDING ADDITIONAL DECK FITTINGS

If you want to add a pad eye or other fitting, such as a cleat, the same procedure applies. Here you may have to reinforce the deck locally in order to mount the pad eye. Figure 2 shows three methods of reinforcing the deck. In *A*, the core material is removed and a plywood insert installed. This operation is performed from the underside of the deck, where it will be hidden by the overhead liner. In *B*, the core is removed altogether, and the two sides of the laminate are joined with extra fiberglass. This is probably the most favored method. Note that if there is no core in the deck, then a large backing plate is essential.

If the new fitting is to have high upward loads, such as a pad eye for a halyard block, you must have some method of securing the fitting against being ripped out of the deck. In *C*, a second pad eye is installed on the back of the first and a tie rod taken from the deck to the cabin sole or to a pad on the back of the mast. This is usually done by the boat manufacturer to secure the mast pad eyes.

IMPROVING THE MAINSHEET SYSTEM

Figure 3 shows a slightly different problem. The mainsheet track is already installed, but it uses stops to hold the mainsheet traveler in place. The owner wants to install tag lines to make the traveler easier to operate. To do this, the first step is to remove the old hardware. Strip the end fittings off the track and remove the stops and traveler. Now the new traveler can be slid onto the track and new end stops bolted into place. The tag line should be spliced to the end stop and led through the traveler, back through the stop to newly installed jamb or cam cleats, as shown in Figure 4. This is a very simple operation and takes only an hour or two. The result is a much-improved mainsheet system.

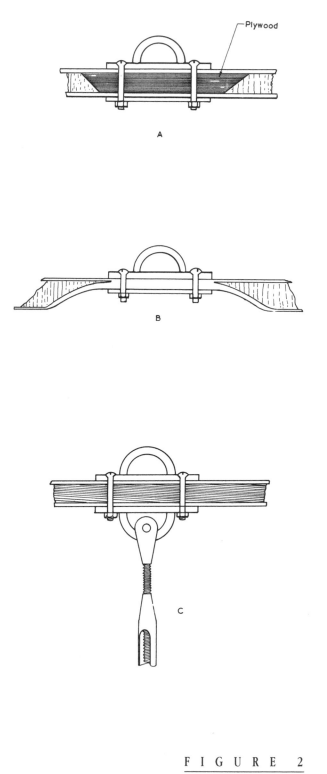

FIGURE 3

Changing the mainsheet track

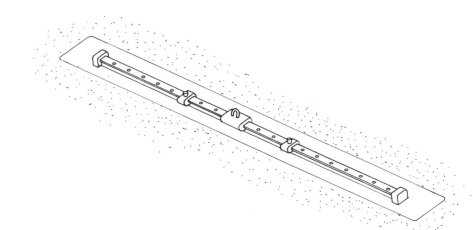

Jamb cleat

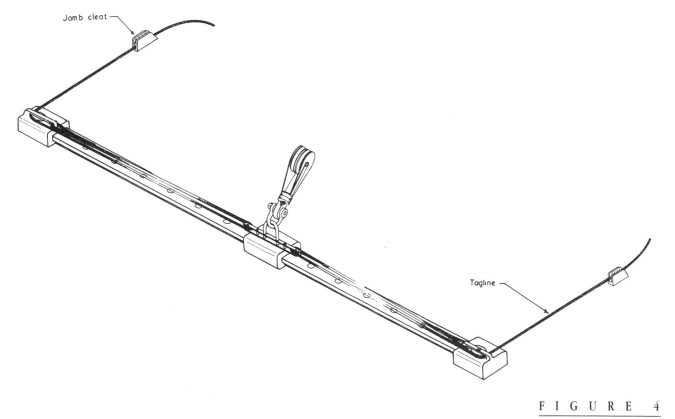

Tagline

FIGURE 4

The new track

PROJECT 3 - 4
INSTALLING A PORTLIGHT

Is the inside of your boat dark and gloomy? If it is, you may want to install an extra portlight to give a little more daylight below. This is not a difficult job and can be accomplished in a few hours.

On the boat illustrated in Figure 1, a port was installed by the builder in the position shown with a solid line. The painted dark stripe disguised the fact that a second port was needed farther forward. After a careful analysis of the interior structure it was found that a second portlight could be installed at the position shown by the dashed line.

Note that this position is not in line with the mast. Under no circumstances should you cut a port directly abeam of the mast. At worst, the strains on the rigging will break the deck at that point. At the very least, the port will leak continuously as the mast and rig work.

With the new portlight's position carefully marked, check the inside of the vessel to make sure you are not about to cut anything structural or to damage furniture. Now drill a hole somewhere inside the marked-out area. Using a jigsaw, cut around the area to be removed. It should come out easily. Clean up the edges of the cut fiberglass with a grinder or file and offer up the port for fitting. Check that the trim plate fits easily. Now caulk all around the fiberglass. Press the port against the caulking to ensure that you get a good seal. If moisture gets into the cut fiberglass, it could cause delamination. Caulk around the flange on the outside of the port to obtain a good seal between the cabin side and the port. Put the port in place as shown in Figure 2 and drill through one of the existing holes in the frame (*B*). If you drill a hole at either end of the port, you can locate it accurately while you drill the other holes. Install the trim plate and hold it in place with one or two bolts. (If the interior liner is cloth or fabric, it should be tucked neatly behind the trim ring. This will give a cleaner, more professional finish to your work.) A section through the port is shown in Figure 3. Note how the parts interlock. Now drill the remaining bolt holes and install the bolts. Before tightening them fully, check that the port

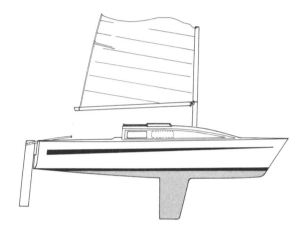

FIGURE 1

The profile of this boat shows the port the builder installed (solid line) and the port the owner intends to install (dashed line).

frame and trim ring are not warped or twisted. They should be perfectly flat.

Tighten the nuts and bolts carefully and saw off any excess bolt. Use a cap nut to make the inside look clean and professional. Use a putty knife to trim off any caulking squeezed out when the trim ring and frame were tightened down. If you wish, you can remove the excess flange and make the inside or outside of the port flush with the face of the trim ring.

Check for watertightness by spraying with a garden hose or pouring a bucket of water over the port. Make sure the drain holes (if any) are not clogged, so that water on the glass of the port drains clear. Now all you have to do is repeat the operation on the other side of the boat.

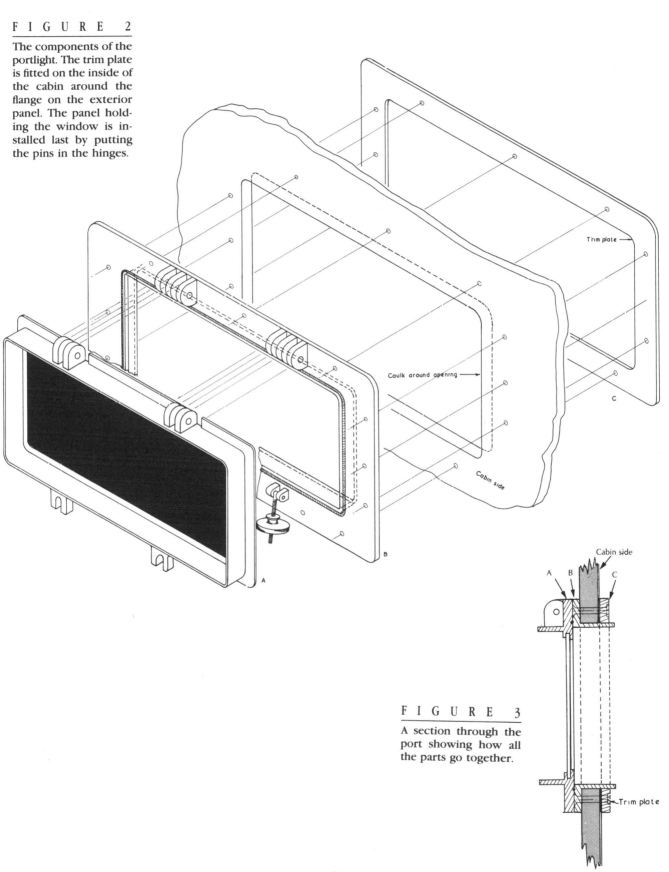

F I G U R E   2

The components of the portlight. The trim plate is fitted on the inside of the cabin around the flange on the exterior panel. The panel holding the window is installed last by putting the pins in the hinges.

Trim plate

Caulk around opening

Cabin side

C

B

A

Cabin side

A   B   C

F I G U R E   3

A section through the port showing how all the parts go together.

Trim plate

PROJECT 3 - 5
ADDING A BOW ROLLER

If you are tired of dragging the anchor out of the bilge and pitching it over the side every time you want to anchor, why not consider a bow roller? It can be used to store the anchor on, it reduces chafe on the anchor line, and makes it easier to retrieve.

Positioning a bow roller and determining the loads on it takes some know-how, so consult the manufacturer. Most are happy to recommend the best size for your boat.

When installing the unit, you should position the roller with the *minimum amount of overhang*. Consider Figure 1. In *A*, the boat is at anchor in calm water and everything is working well. In *B*, the boat is at anchor under storm conditions. Waves are rolling through the harbor and the scend is quite large. The anchor line is pulling downward and the buoyancy of the yacht is forcing the bow upward. Something has to give. In this situation, it is likely to be the anchor roller, which may pull out of the deck, leaving a gaping hole. In severe weather the boat might even sink.

In Figure 2 the anchor roller is positioned as far aft as possible. In this case the problem is the point of the anchor hitting the bow of the boat (shown with an arrow). A compromise has to be made. The roller extension over the bow should be as short as possible but not so short that the anchor hits the boat. Other than that, you can put the roller anywhere on the boat. In the BOC challenge, the single-handed race around the world, one competitor had twin anchor rollers, one on each quarter. This allowed him to stream warps or a sea anchor to slow the boat in extremely high winds.

Figure 3 shows how a bow roller is installed. It is through-bolted through the deck and a backing plate. The thickness of the backing plate should be the same thickness as the plating of the bow roller. Each bolt should be backed with large washers and double-nutted. This should prevent the nuts vibrating loose and allowing the anchor roller to drop off or droop.

FIGURE 1

A large amount of overhang will cause the roller to bend or snap off if the boat is anchored during severe conditions.

FIGURE 2

Setting the bow roller too far aft will cause it to hit the boat when the anchor is hoisted.

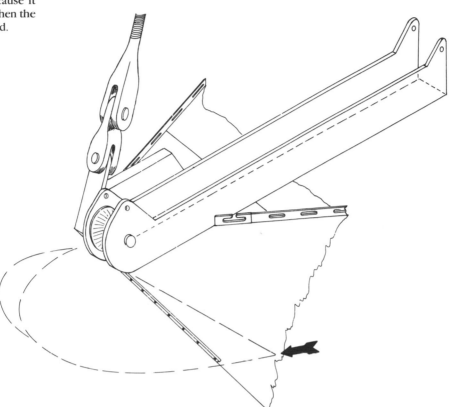

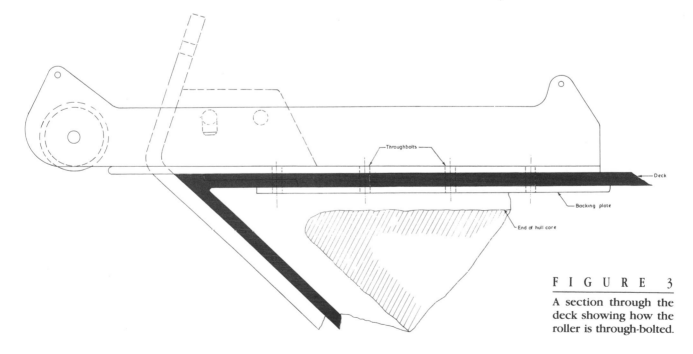

FIGURE 3

A section through the deck showing how the roller is through-bolted.

P R O J E C T   3 - 6
REPAIRING OR REPLACING CHAIN PLATES

Occasionally, often disastrously a chain plate will pull out from the side of the hull. If that happens, you will have to repair it before the boat will be usable again. Here we look at installing chain plates.

Before you can change the chain plate layout on your boat, you will have to measure carefully back from the bow and from the centerline of the hull—not the side of the mast—to ensure that the chain plates are correctly located. Figure 1 shows how this is done. Measure the distance Y from the tack fitting and the distance X from the centerline to the position of the chain plate. They should be the same on both sides of the boat.

Figure 2 shows how the chain plates should be aligned when being installed. They should be in line with the vertical and diagonal shroud. Because the mast moves around in the boat, all the transverse chain plates at the deck should have toggles, so alignment need not be perfect, but it should be close.

When installing the chain plates make sure they line up carefully with the angles of the vertical and diagonal shrouds. A chain plate not lined up correctly will soon break.

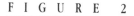

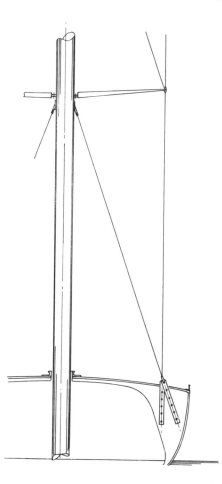

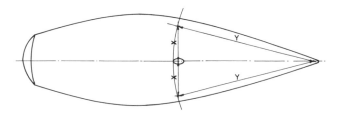

F I G U R E   1
If you should decide to change the rigging lay-out of your boat, you may have to reposition the chain plates. First you will need to measure very carefully to locate their position. Measure back from the tack the distance Y and scribe an arc. At the chain-plate position the distance X to the center of the mast should be equal on both sides of the boat.

There are many methods of installing chain plates. Figures 3, 4, and 5 show some of them. Figure 3 shows the chain plate bolted to a bulkhead in way of the mast. This is a fairly well-used method, but remember to install a backing plate on the other side of the bulkhead. The installation shown in Figure 4 is often used on smaller craft and dinghies. The U-shaped chain plate is pushed through a rod under the coaming and bolted from underneath. Care should be taken to ensure that the nuts are locked tightly. A nut dropping off while you are under way could be disastrous! On narrower vessels the chain plates were often bolted to the outside of the hull. Figure 5 shows the installation. This is a simple method, but care should be taken to ensure that the inside of the hull is securely braced. Either install blocking to spread the load or bolt through a frame and add backing plates.

On fiberglass boats the chain plates are usually bolted to glass brackets securely fastened to the inside of the hull as shown in Figure 6. The bracket is made out of plywood and securely encapsulated inside the fiberglass. If you choose this method, then make sure the glasswork is of high quality and that backing plates are used.

While installing a chain plate may seem like a big job, you will be surprised how easy it can be. Before you go to the yard, take a look to see how much you can do. You may save yourself substantial amounts of money for little effort.

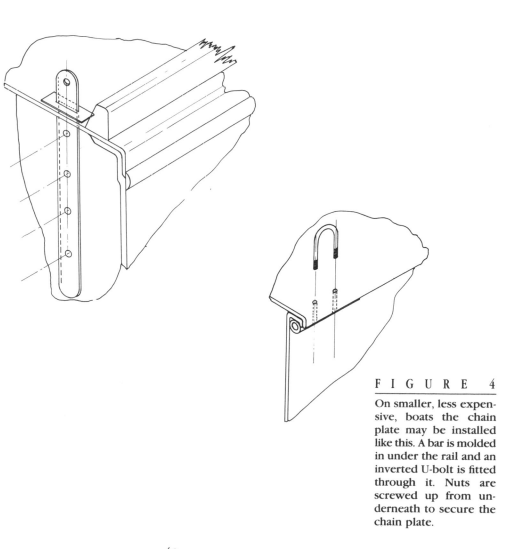

F I G U R E   3

On many boats the chain plates are bolted to the bulkhead in way of the mast. Note that this arrangement will require a backing plate on the other side of the bulkhead.

F I G U R E   4

On smaller, less expensive, boats the chain plate may be installed like this. A bar is molded in under the rail and an inverted U-bolt is fitted through it. Nuts are screwed up from underneath to secure the chain plate.

49

F I G U R E   5

On a narrow boat the chain plate is often bolted onto the outside of the hull. If this is done, care must be taken to ensure that the chain plate is thoroughly caulked and sealed to prevent leakage.

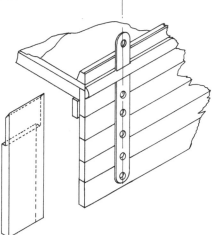

F I G U R E   6

Many glass boats have the chain plates bolted to substantial brackets glassed into the inside of the hull. If you intend to use this method, you should probably use plywood as the filler piece for the chain plate and use a backing plate on the other side of the installation.

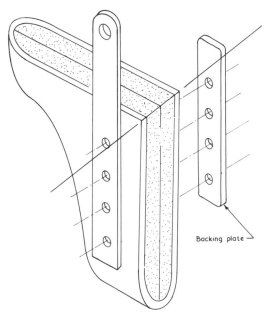

Backing plate

CHAPTER 4

INTERIOR
MODIFICATIONS

One of the most popular areas for modification is the boat's interior. There are so many small changes to the interior that can add up to major improvements. For instance, a fold-down table beside your berth might make it easier to set your book or morning coffee down. A shelf converted into a locker gives more storage space. Steps under the companionway ladder can be transformed into tool stowage. This chapter contains many ideas that you can modify to suit your boat. The list is long, and while some projects are easy, others require more skill. Choose easy projects first and, as your skill improves, tackle the larger jobs.

PROJECT 4-1
A STANDARD FOLD-DOWN
BULKHEAD-MOUNTED TABLE

Constructing a bulkhead-mounted table is one of the larger jobs, but it is shown first because a boat's table is one of the most often-changed items in the interior. If there is not enough space in the middle of a boat for a large table, or if your present table gets in the way of folding sails, you might want to add a folding table. The ideal table could be a bulkhead-mounted unit that folds out of the way when not in use. This drawing shows the details of such a table.

First decide upon the length of the table. As the height of most tables is 29 inches (767 mm), this dimension becomes a critical one in your choice of table type. If the table is to be less than 29 inches (767 mm) long, you can easily construct a fold-down table as shown in Figure 3, which shows the profile of the standard fold-down table. Note how the leg will fold up under the top before the unit is lowered against the bulkhead. If the table is to be longer than 29 inches (767 mm), a fold-down table becomes a problem. However, by making the table fold upward, as shown in

Figure 4, its length is restricted only by the height of the cabin headroom. In other words, if the table is to be 29 inches (767 mm) high, and the distance from the cabin sole to the deckhead is 74 inches (1.88 m), the table can be $74 - 29 = 45$ inches ($1880 - 767 = 1113$ mm) long and it will still fold upward against the bulkhead. If you want a slightly higher or lower table, adjust the length accordingly.

CUTTING OUT THE TABLE SURFACE

Measure the width and the length you want. The ideal width varies according to the boat, but should not be more than the distance from the cushion face on the port side to the cushion face on the starboard side less $\frac{3}{8}$ inch (9.5 mm). Figure 1 shows the dimensions. We will assume that our table is to be 28 inches (711 mm) wide and 29 inches (767 mm) long.

The first step is to cut a pattern for the tabletop out of a piece of scrap cardboard and try it in the boat. Use a piece of drafting or duct tape to hold the cardboard to the bulkhead where the table will be fitted. Remember to add on extra distance to allow for the thickness of the mounting blocks. Raise and lower the cardboard, making sure it will clear any seats or other obstructions.

Now cut the tabletop out of plywood to the dimensions shown in Figure 2. The usual material for tabletops is $\frac{3}{4}$-inch (18 mm) marine-grade plywood. If light weight is required, you can use $\frac{1}{2}$-inch (12 mm) ply, or even make up a laminated tabletop using a core material such as Hexcel™ and $\frac{1}{8}$-inch (3 mm) ply, or a light veneer on the bottom with a laminate on top. If you laminate only on one side, the table may warp.

The dashed lines in Figure 2 show the layout of material and the edge trim used for this unit. Once you have cut out the top, clean up the edges and edge-band them with $\frac{3}{4}$-inch (18 mm) banding tape. On a conventional table you might want to make fancy fiddles and edge banding as shown in Project 4-8: Installing Fiddles and Sea Rails. If light weight is desired, a simple $\frac{3}{4}$-inch-wide (18 mm) edge-banding tape epoxied in place is a viable solution.

SUPPORTING THE TABLE

Now you need to support the table. You will need a leg and a bulkhead bracket. The leg can be laid out as in Figure 1 and cut out of $\frac{3}{4}$-inch (18 mm) marine-grade plywood. If you use plywood, it should be edge-banded. As an alternative a $\frac{3}{4}$-inch by 8-inch (18 mm $\times$ 200 mm) solid-wood plank will give an old-fashioned look to your table. If light weight is desired, cut out the center of the leg as shown by the dashed line.

You will also need a piano hinge the same length as the bulkhead bracket and another the same length as the top of the supporting leg. Use screws sized to fit the piano hinges but not longer than $\frac{3}{4}$ inch (18 mm). They can be mounted as shown in Figures 1A and 1B.

The supporting element is the bulkhead bracket, which is cut out of wood, as shown in Figure 1A. The dimensions are critical. The hinge centerline should be at least $2\frac{1}{4}$ inches (56 mm) from the bulkhead to allow the table and leg to fold up flush. A $\frac{1}{4}$-inch (6 mm) bolt is shown holding the table to the bulkhead, but you can make a neater job by gluing and screwing the bracket to the bulkhead. If you use bolts, put a backing plate on the other side of the bulkhead. This can then be covered with a piece of molding or trim.

To secure the leg, fit it into a piece of molding glued and screwed to the cabin sole. While this is easier to make than the brass plate shown in 1D, it does have a tendency to be tripped over. Figure 1C shows a section through the molding. Note how it is shaped for minimum height and has a deep groove to hold the table leg.

Another method of securing the leg is to use a pin in its bottom face to locate it in the cabin sole. You can make the pin from a $2\frac{1}{2}$-inch (60 mm) brass wood screw as shown in Figure 1D. Screw it into the bottom of the leg until all the threads are covered. Then saw off the head with a hacksaw, leaving about an inch of unthreaded brass to project. This will become the pin. Use a file to take off any burrs, and the pin is now ready to use.

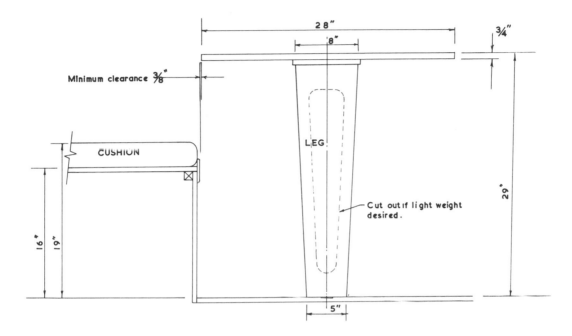

Typical dimensions of a
cabin table showing bunk
height and leg.

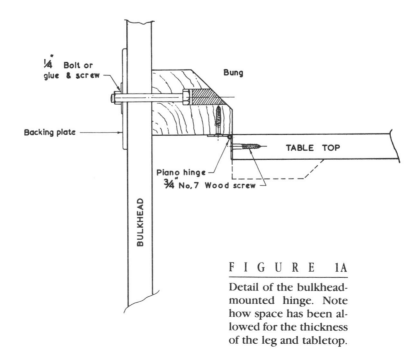

F I G U R E   1A

Detail of the bulkhead-
mounted hinge. Note
how space has been al-
lowed for the thickness
of the leg and tabletop.

ASSEMBLING THE TABLE

The first step in assembling the table is to mount the leg on the underside. First mount the wood block shown in Figure 1B to the underside of the table, then screw the hinge to the block. You are only locating the hinge at this time, so you just need to insert a couple of screws. At this stage the table should be assembled without gluing so as to ensure that it both fits and works properly. When everything is assembled and it all works, the wood parts can be permanently glued and screwed together. Next screw the hinge to the leg, again using only two or three screws, and check that it folds properly. If it works satisfactorily, you can proceed with mounting the table on the bulkhead.

The first step in mounting the table is to screw the piano hinge to the tabletop, as shown in Figure 1A. You might want to reinforce the tabletop at this point by adding a wooden block under the table end, as shown by the dashed line. Next drill the holes for the hinge, but do not screw it down until you have mounted the bracket on the bulkhead. Measure carefully up from the cabin sole to obtain a line parallel to the sole before screwing the bracket to the bulkhead. (If the bulkhead is less than ½-inch (12 mm) plywood, you may have to use bolts and put a backing plate on the other side of the bulkhead.) When the bracket is firmly screwed in place,

all the holes should be filled or bunged and sanded. Now screw the hinge in place. If you want a very professional appearance, locate the hinge where it will not be seen when the table is in use. Finally, carefully lower the table and locate the pinhole or molding position for the leg. If you use molding, be sure it is straight and screw it in place. If you use a brass plate, you can either chisel out a recess for the plate, drill a hole for the pin, and mount everything flush with the top of the sole, or you can screw the plate to the cabin sole after drilling a hole for the pin. A flush-mounted plate looks much more professional and will not be an obstacle to crew walking past.

THE UPWARD-FOLDING TABLE

In most boats bunks are just over 6 feet (1.8 m) long. As bunks often become settees during the daytime and the table is intended to sit the entire crew, the cabin table may also be quite long. Even if we allow two feet for a crewman to slide into the seat, the table will be about 4 feet (1.219 m) long. This makes it difficult to fold downward against the bulkhead. It can only be folded downward if it were made to be hinged in the middle. It can be folded upward, however, and you should assess your own space to see if this is more convenient.

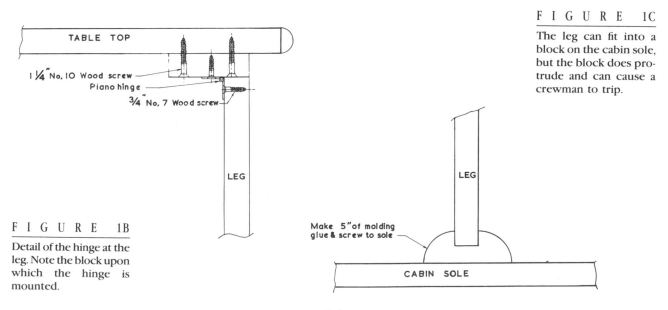

TABLE TOP

1 ¼" No. 10 Wood screw

Piano hinge

¾" No. 7 Wood screw

LEG

FIGURE 1B

Detail of the hinge at the leg. Note the block upon which the hinge is mounted.

Make 5" of molding glue & screw to sole

LEG

CABIN SOLE

FIGURE 1C

The leg can fit into a block on the cabin sole, but the block does protrude and can cause a crewman to trip.

FIGURE 1D

A better method is to recess a brass plate into the cabin sole and make a pin to fit the plate. The pin can be made from a wood screw with the head cut off.

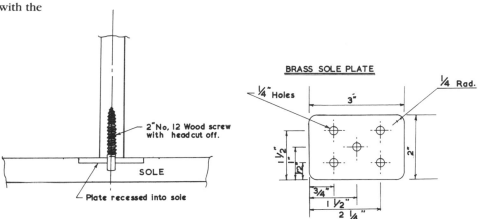

BRASS SOLE PLATE

2" No, 12 Wood screw with head cut off.

SOLE

Plate recessed into sole

¼" Holes   3"   ¼ Rad.

1 ½"   ½"   2"

¾"   1 ½"   2 ¼"

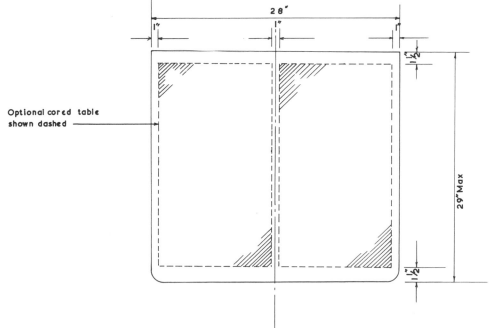

28"

1"   1"   1"

Optional cored table shown dashed

1 ½"   29" Max   1 ½"

FIGURE 2

Typical table dimensions. If you want to make a lightweight table, then a core should be inserted in the shaded area.

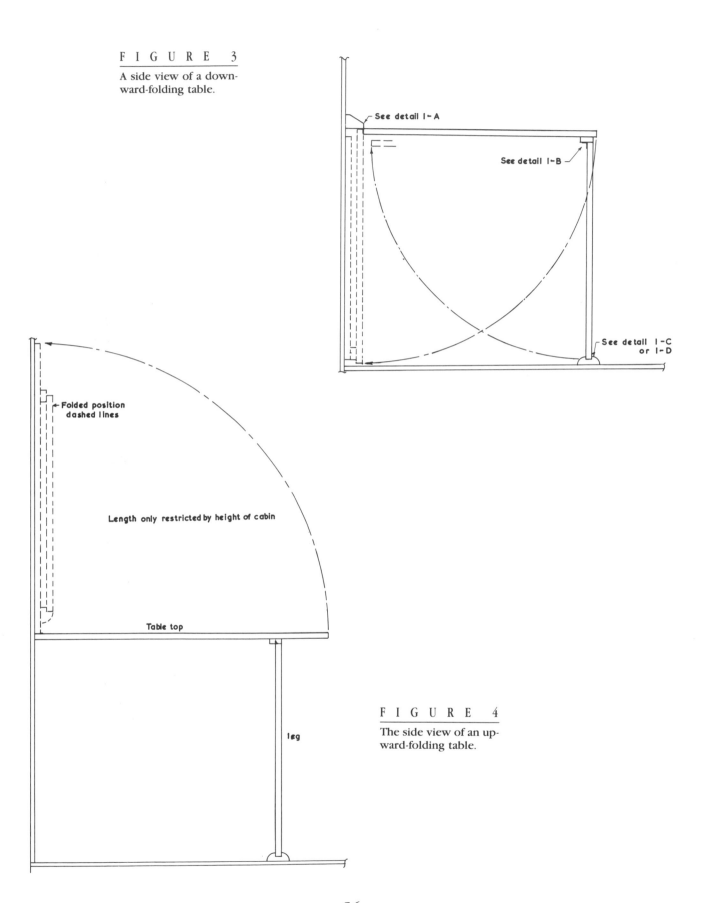

F I G U R E 3

A side view of a down-ward-folding table.

See detail I~A

See detail I~B

See detail I~C
or I~D

← Folded position
dashed lines

Length only restricted by height of cabin

Table top

leg

F I G U R E 4

The side view of an up-ward-folding table.

PROJECT 4-2
A FOLD-AWAY TABLE LONGER THAN 29 INCHES (767 MM)

Suppose you have decided to fit a bulkhead-mounted table longer than 29 inches (767 mm), but the boat does not have the headroom to allow it to fold upward. You have two possible solutions. One is to make the bulkhead end of the table slide down for storage. The other is to make the table totally removable. The sliding table uses either two specially made pieces of 1-inch by 1/8-inch (25-mm × 3-mm) stainless steel or brass plate, or two pieces of mainsail track to enable the table to move up and down. Figure 1 shows the fold-away table in the open position and Figure 2 shows it in the stowed position.

CUTTING OUT THE MATERIALS

Cut out the tabletop and leg and fit them in exactly the same manner as described for the previous bulkhead-mounted table. It is the method of attaching the table to the bulkhead that is different. First, make two moldings, shown as A on Figure 3. These moldings will be mounted vertically on the bulkhead. Next you will need two pieces of stainless steel or brass flat bar 1 inch by 1/8-inch (25 mm × 3 mm). These are attached to the molding as shown in Figure 4. You may want to make the table serve a dual purpose and become part of a double bunk. If so, the height will need to be adjustable. You can do this by drilling several holes in the flat bar to locate the retaining pin. Then you must make an adjustable leg for the table—usually a telescopic tubular leg. Figure 5 shows a typical one. The molding on the bulkhead end of the table will also be different from that on the previous table. Rather than mounting the molding directly to the bulkhead, you will need to attach slides to each end.

These slides fit in the slots created by the vertical pieces of stainless steel and are held in place by the retaining pins. Figure 6 gives the dimensions of a typical table.

ASSEMBLING THE SLIDING TABLE

Mount the leg on the underside of the table in the same manner described for the fold-down bulkhead-mounted table. Next locate the positions of the vertical moldings. If you are unsure that the table will work properly, or if tolerances are very small, hang the moldings on the bulkhead with one or two screws and continue with the assembly. The moldings can be glued and screwed in their final position after assembly is complete and everything is adjusted carefully. One stainless steel strip can now be screwed to the vertical molding. Before fitting the second strip, put the table in position with the slides fitted in the slots created by the vertical molding and steel strip. Now screw on the other stainless strip. This will hold the table firmly to the bulkhead. Adjust the height as required and drill the hole for the pin. Fold the table against the bulkhead and check that everything works properly and nothing binds. If you are making an adjustable table, it should be tried in all its positions before the final dismantling and reassembly, when all the parts are glued and screwed in their respective positions.

Mounting the table on slides also makes the table more versatile. The bulkhead end can be lowered until the other end drops into a fitting at bunk level, allowing the table to be converted into a double bunk. (See the section on bunks at the end of this chapter.)

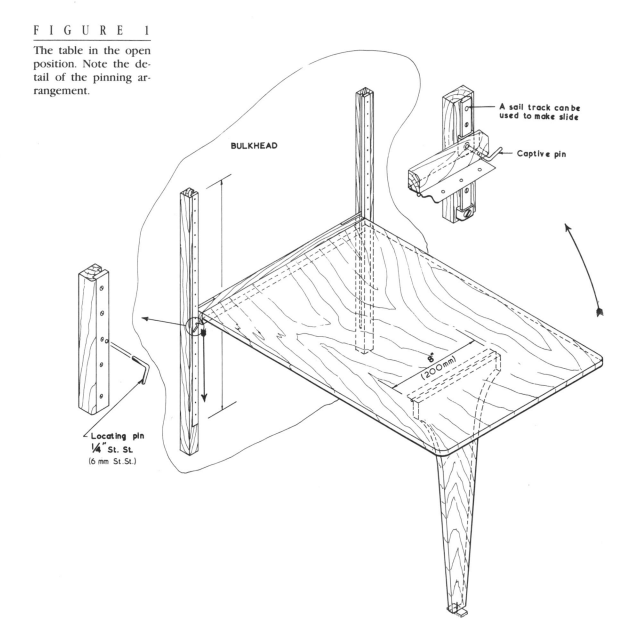

FIGURE 1

The table in the open position. Note the detail of the pinning arrangement.

BULKHEAD

A sail track can be used to make slide

Captive pin

8" (200mm)

Locating pin ¼" St. St. (6 mm St.St.)

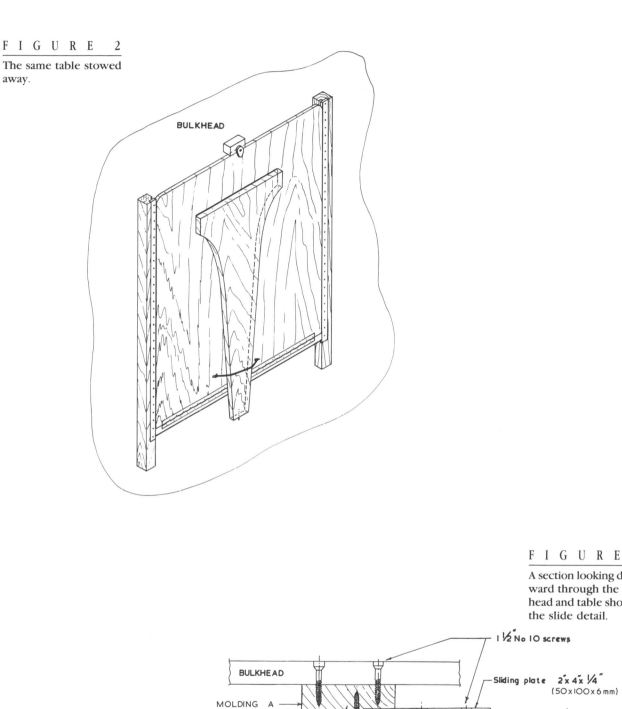

FIGURE 2

The same table stowed away.

BULKHEAD

FIGURE 3

A section looking downward through the bulkhead and table showing the slide detail.

1½" No 10 screws

BULKHEAD

Sliding plate 2"x 4"x ¼"
(50x100x6mm)

MOLDING   A

(75x30mm)3"x 1¼" molding
(25x 3 mm)1"x ⅛" St. St. strip

Table mounting molding

59

F I G U R E   4

The table ready to be mounted on the sliding part.

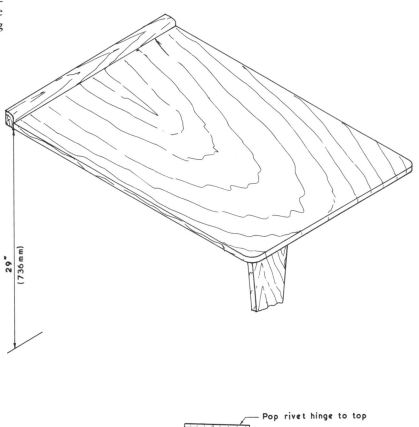

29" (736 mm)

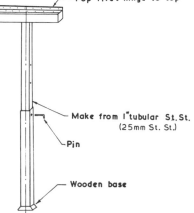

Pop rivet hinge to top

Make from 1" tubular St.St. (25mm St. St.)

Pin

Wooden base

F I G U R E   5

If the table is to be part of a bunk or needs to be adjustable in height, then an adjustable leg should be made, as shown here.

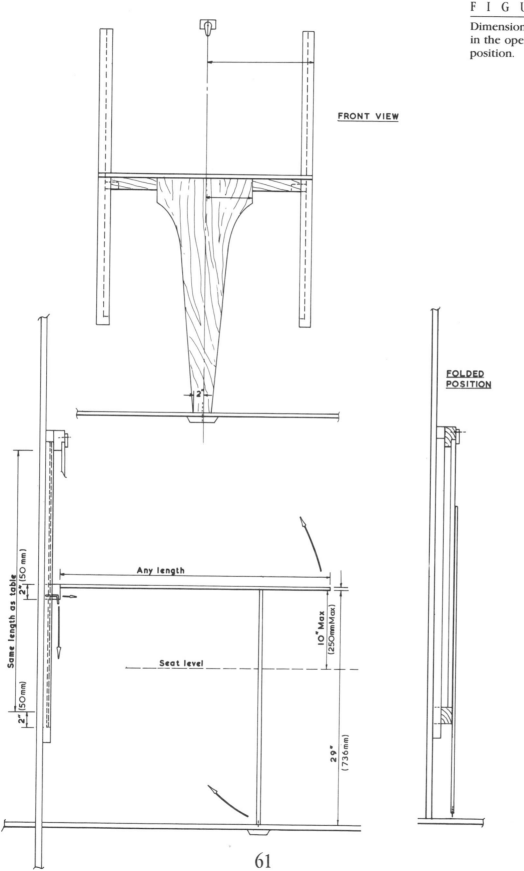

FRONT VIEW

FOLDED
POSITION

Any length

Same length as table

2" (50 mm)

2" (50 mm)

2"

10" Max
(250mm Max)

Seat level

29"
(736mm)

F I G U R E   6
Dimensions of the table
in the open and closed
position.

PROJECT 4 - 3
A GIMBALLED TABLE

Quite often you see a gimballed table in a yacht and think that it would be a useful addition to your boat. This drawing shows a gimballed table. Figure 1 shows it in the closed position. (One leaf is removed for clarity.) This table has several useful features. There is space for cutlery and condiments in a special compartment in the middle leaf. There is also a shelf for napkins and towels underneath. If you want to put bottles in this rack, the sides should be higher, or you can make a hinge-down flap on one side and divide the storage space into compartments for bottles.

Figure 2 shows the same table in the open position. The top is set on the stand and is free to swing through an arc of about 20 degrees either side of horizontal. A gimballed table requires some reasonably heavy weights bolted to the underside of the bottom shelf to slow the rate of swing. Or you can put the weights on the shelf and firmly secure them in place.

Figures 3 and 4 show the side and end views of the same table. Note that a pin should be provided if desired to stop the table from swinging. More sophisticated tables have a braking mechanism to slow down the rate of swing, but on this table the same effect can be achieved by adding more weights.

F I G U R E   1

A drop-leaf gimballed table in the closed position. One leaf has been removed for clarity.

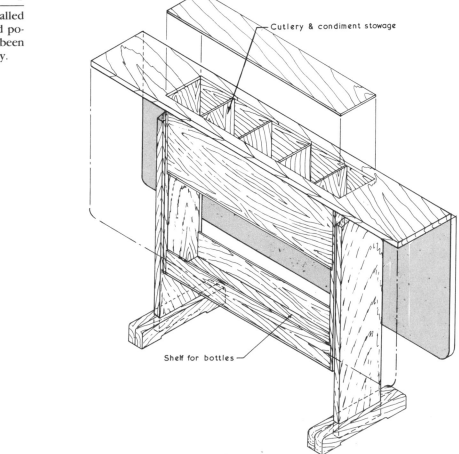

Cutlery & condiment stowage

Shelf for bottles

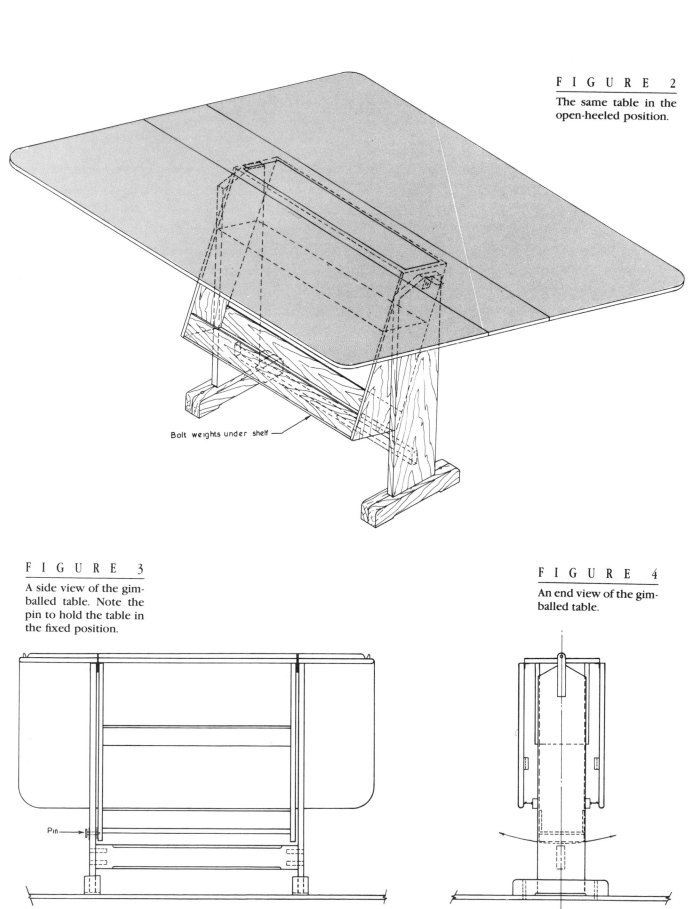

Bolt weights under shelf

F I G U R E   3

A side view of the gimballed table. Note the pin to hold the table in the fixed position.

Pin

F I G U R E   4

An end view of the gimballed table.

PROJECT 4-4
A GIMBALLED LEAF TABLE

Quite often the leaf on the windward side of a gimballed table bangs on the knees of the diners, while the leaf on the low side is about chest level. The table shown in this drawing reduces that problem by allowing the leaves to swivel independently of the middle portion.

The two outside leaves are mounted at the end of a pivot arm, which is attached to the table's pedestal as shown in Figure 1. Note that the pivot arm must be set well below the level of the tabletop to ensure that it misses the leaf when the leaf is canted on the high side. This problem is indicated by the arrow in Figure 2. Figure 3 shows a section through the pivot point. Note the large piece of lead used as the counterbalance. This lead, which should weigh at least 10 pounds (5 kgs) at each end, will have to be positioned carefully to get the best balance. It would be best to make the leaf-support arm X quite long and move the lead up or down until the ideal balance is found. Only then should the support arm be trimmed. All linkages should be through-bolted fairly tightly to provide some measure of damping to the moving parts.

However, if not properly developed, this table does have a somewhat cranky motion. This project is best undertaken by a person with some woodworking and boatbuilding skills. Note, too, that while these drawings indicate the principles of such a table, they are not to scale and do not indicate specific dimensions.

FIGURE 1

The table in the open position.

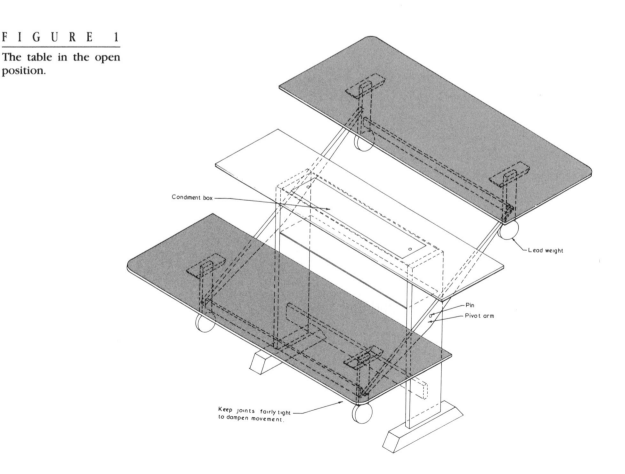

Condiment box

Lead weight

Pin

Pivot arm

Keep joints fairly tight to dampen movement.

F I G U R E   2

An end view of the ta-
ble. When the boat is
heeled, there may be
contact at the point ar-
rowed. Care must be
taken to ensure that the
dimensions are laid out
carefully in order to
avoid this contact if
possible.

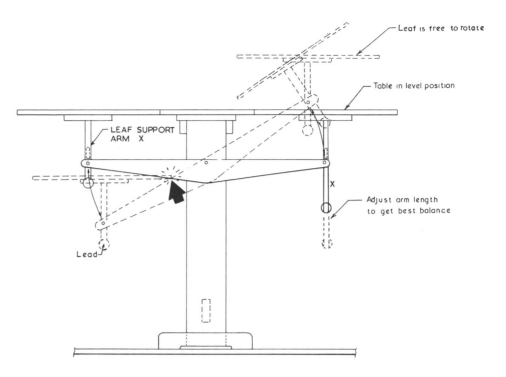

LEAF SUPPORT
ARM X

Leaf is free to rotate

Table in level position

X

Adjust arm length
to get best balance

Lead

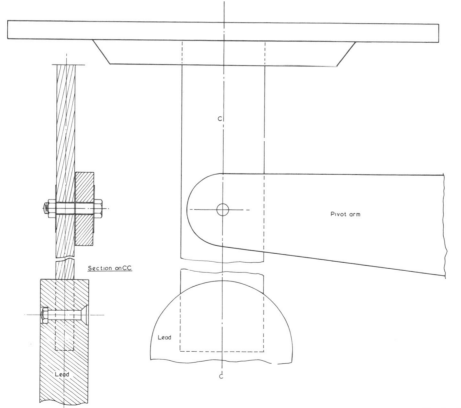

Section on CC

Lead

C

Pivot arm

C

Lead

F I G U R E   3

Large-scale detail of the
gimballing mechanism.

PROJECT 4 - 5
A CONVENTIONAL DROP-LEAF TABLE

The drop-leaf table is probably the most common table on larger boats and can easily be scaled down to suit smaller craft. The table has a center section firmly fixed to the cabin sole, often containing lockers for condiments, cutlery, or bottles of wine. Two leaves are hinged off the center section. When not in use, they fold down and are fastened tightly. When the table is to be used, the leaves are raised and arms locked in place underneath to support them. Figure 1 shows a typical table with wine lockers fitted in the middle section (dashed lines) and a leaf removed for clarity. Figure 2 shows

one variation with a round top. A drop-leaf table can be made to suit any space, and the shape is limited only by what will fit and by your imagination.

Figures 3 and 4 show the profile and side views of the table in Figure 1. Note the catch that holds the leaves when they are lowered. Notice also the block (B) in Figure 3 which adds a little height to the leaf to ensure that it does not sag. The footrest (F) in Figure 4 can be left as a footrest or can be modified to become a shelf or even lockers.

FIGURE 1

A typical drop-leaf table showing details of the well in the middle of the table.

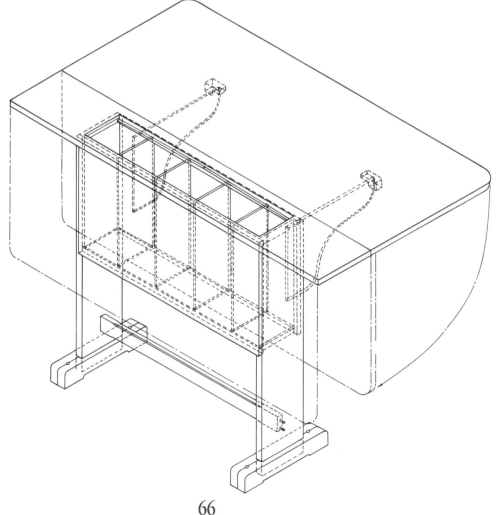

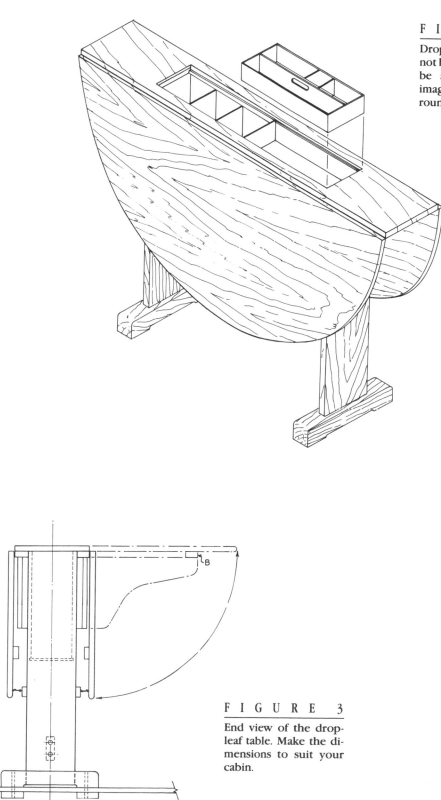

F I G U R E   2
Drop-leaf tables need not be square. They can be almost any shape imaginable. This one is round.

F I G U R E   3
End view of the drop-leaf table. Make the dimensions to suit your cabin.

F I G U R E   4
Side view of the table.
Note the bevel on the
footrail.

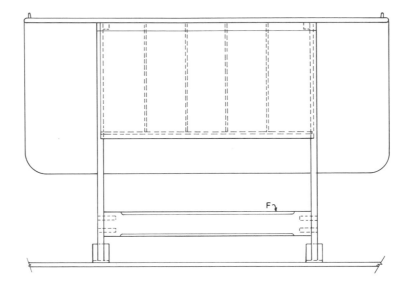

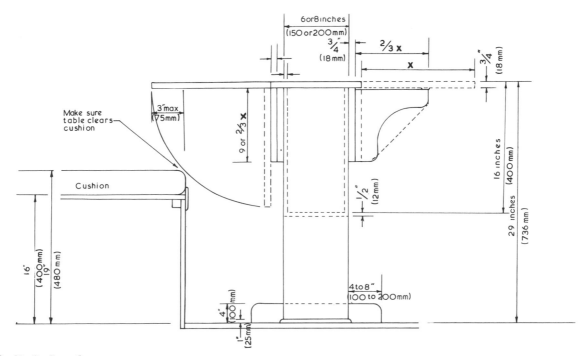

F I G U R E   5

The dimensions of the
table, showing how it
works with a seat.

FIGURE 6

Dimensions of the tabletop. The length and leaf width can be adjusted to suit your cabin.

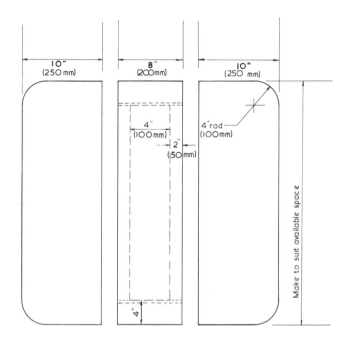

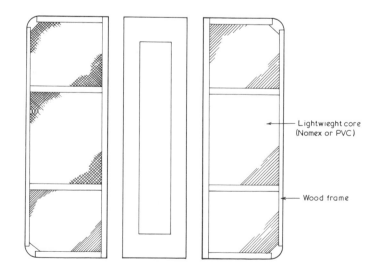

Lightwieght core (Nomex or PVC)

Wood frame

FIGURE 7

If you wish to make a lightweight table, the top can be laid out as shown here. A core material such as Nomex or Klegecell is bonded between two layers of ⅛-inch (3-mm) plywood.

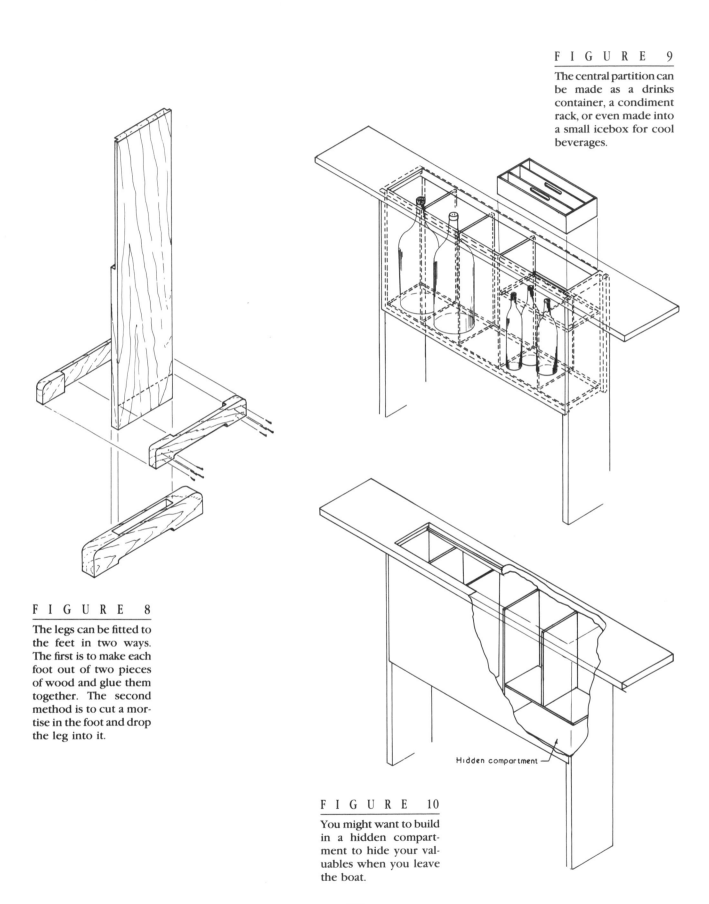

F I G U R E   9

The central partition can be made as a drinks container, a condiment rack, or even made into a small icebox for cool beverages.

F I G U R E   8

The legs can be fitted to the feet in two ways. The first is to make each foot out of two pieces of wood and glue them together. The second method is to cut a mortise in the foot and drop the leg into it.

Hidden compartment

F I G U R E   10

You might want to build in a hidden compartment to hide your valuables when you leave the boat.

LAYING OUT THE TABLE

Figure 5 shows dimensions for an average-size dining table. In this case the leaves are 10 inches (250 mm) wide, but they can be as wide as the table is tall. In other words, you could make each leaf 28½ inches (724 mm) wide if you made a 29-inch-high (736 mm) table. However, you should remember to check the clearance between seats and the leaves as they are folded. As Figure 1 shows, the maximum distance is 3 inches (75 mm). The supports for the leaf should be about two-thirds of the length of the leaf in order to support it properly. Note that the support is completely concealed by the leaf when the latter is folded down.

Most tabletops are ¾-inch (18 mm) thick. However, if you are making a smaller table, you could use ½-inch (12 mm) plywood. The tabletop dimensions are shown in Figure 6. Figure 7 shows how the top of the table can be made from high-tech materials if an extremely light unit is required. This one has ¾-inch (18 mm) Nomex (an aramid honeycomb material made by Du Pont) as the core with ¾-inch by 2-inch (18 mm × 50 mm) edging. The edging is required to fasten hinges and catches.

Figure 8 shows how the legs and feet go together. There are two options. The first is to clamp the leg between two pieces of specially shaped wood. These feet are glued and screwed together. The other option is to cut a mortise in the foot and slot the leg into it. While this is a better, stronger method, it is more time-consuming and calls for a greater level of skill.

The opening in the middle section can be used for many things. In Figure 9 it is used as a wine locker with a small space for the bottle opener and other bar utensils. Some people prefer to keep cutlery in this compartment, others use it for flashlights. Whatever you decide to use it for, be sure to size the compartments to the size of the object to be stored.

Figure 10 offers a different option. In this design the bottle rack has a secret compartment, which can be used to store valuables and money if you have to leave the boat for a short time. If you decide to make a hidden compartment, be sure you have disguised the way in. If you can see it, so can a thief!

THE EXPLODED VIEW

When all the parts are carefully measured and ready to put together, they are assembled as shown in this exploded view. The parts are labeled and listed in the parts list. All parts should be carefully dry-fitted and then glued and screwed. Remember to clamp assembled parts firmly to ensure a good fit. In Figure 11, the exploded view shows the various parts of the table. To assemble, first assemble the middle section by clamping the end pieces (H) to the crosspieces (K and L). Part K, the footrest, is doweled on this drawing, but you can cut a mortise in the leg and fit it a little tighter.

Next add the one side of the box (G). The grooves are either routed out or cut on a table saw. Align the partitions (N) with this side and install the other side. Glue and screw the cleats (M) to the underside of the tabletop (P) and then install the tabletop on the assembled box. Carefully align part C and locate the hinge. (The hinge can be temporarily installed by inserting screws at either end to hold it in place.) Now the table cleats (F), hinges (E), and supports (D) can be installed. Note how the supports (D) are fastened to spacer cleats (F) to allow the tabletop leaves to fold down over them easily. Next add the leaves. Again, they can be temporarily installed with two or three screws in order to ensure the assembled unit works easily without binding. When you are satisfied with the fit, the entire leaf-support assembly should be glued and screwed tightly in place.

The tabletop insert (Q) fits into the hole in the tabletop, but note how the two parts (O) are tapered so that pressure on one end of Q will tip it up and allow it to be lifted out of the slot. The feet (J) should be installed last. These should be glued and screwed to the bottom of the legs, as shown here. This will complete the assembly of the drop-leaf table.

F I G U R E 11

An exploded view of the
conventional table.

PROJECT 4-6
INSTALLING FIDDLES AND SEA RAILS

A grizzled old seaman once asked me if I knew the difference between a fiddle and a sea rail. I didn't, and he explained that a fiddle rail is nonremovable, whereas a sea rail is removable and is only used when the boat is at sea. In this project various examples of fiddles and sea rails are shown. Fiddles are positioned around the edge of almost every countertop or table on a boat. Figure 1 shows a drop-leaf table. It may have fiddles around the edges of each leaf and around the middle portion to keep items in place when the leaves are folded. Any or all of the rails may be removable. I've seen some boats where every rail could be removed. On other craft all the rails are glued and screwed in place.

Height is of critical importance to a fiddle. If a low fiddle is fitted, a plate may ride up and over it. Figure 2 shows the ideal height. It stops plates from riding over, but doesn't quite reach the cup handle.

Figure 3 shows some different types of fiddle rails. A is a solid rail, as seen on many modern vessels. B is made with small, concave posts. Each post has a small dowel on either end to enable it to be inserted into a small hole in the fiddle rail. The shapes of each post are shown in the column labeled shape of post. The fatter posts shown in C are spaced farther apart than the ones in B. D shows posts made from dowel rods. If you decide to make your own posts, this is a simple way of doing it.

Corners pose special problems for fiddle rails. I like to end the rail before the corner wherever possible. If the fiddle is taken to the corner, it is quite difficult to clean the corner, and grime tends to accumulate there. Wet grime will eventually rot the corner of the fiddle rail. In Figure 4, A shows how conventional solid fiddles are ended. If you are an expert at laminating wood, the treatment shown in B is very attractive. Here the fiddle is molded around the corner, and a slot is cut out with either a router or saw. The bottom of the slot is flush with the countertop. In C the old-fashioned fiddle is very attractive if it is bent around the corner, leaving room underneath to clean the countertop.

Figure 5 shows how to make a removable solid rail. Insert a wood screw into the rail and cut its head off, leaving a stub about ¾-inch (18 mm) long. Thin brass tubing is inserted into holes drilled into the table. The inside diameter of the tubing should match the exterior diameter of the screws so that the rail will easily drop into place. Note that the bottoms of the brass tubes are left open to allow crumbs and grime to drop through.

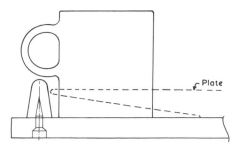

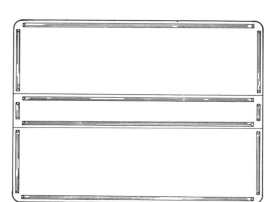

FIGURE 1

The layout of fiddles on a drop-leaf table. Quite often the rails on the middle portion of the table are removable.

FIGURE 2

The rail should not be high enough to hit the cup handle but should be high enough to stop a plate sliding over it.

F I G U R E 3

Details of various fiddle rails. A is a solid rail. B and C use turned posts. Note the difference in spacing of the thin and fat posts. D uses pieces of dowel and can be made up very simply.

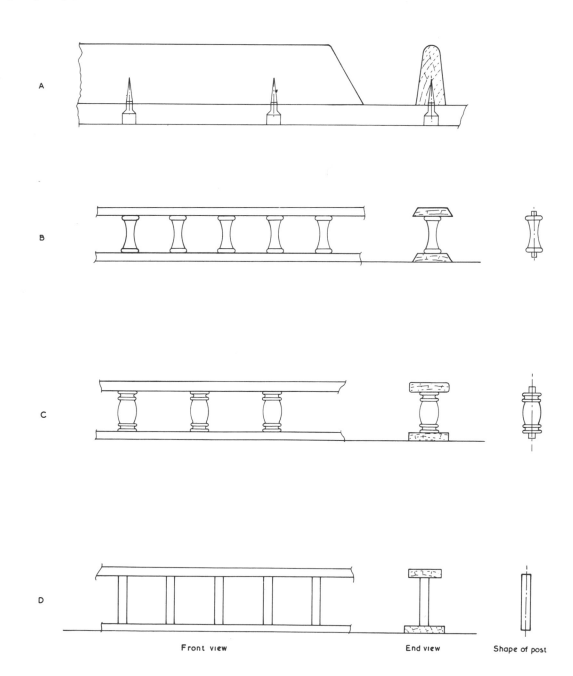

Front view   End view   Shape of post

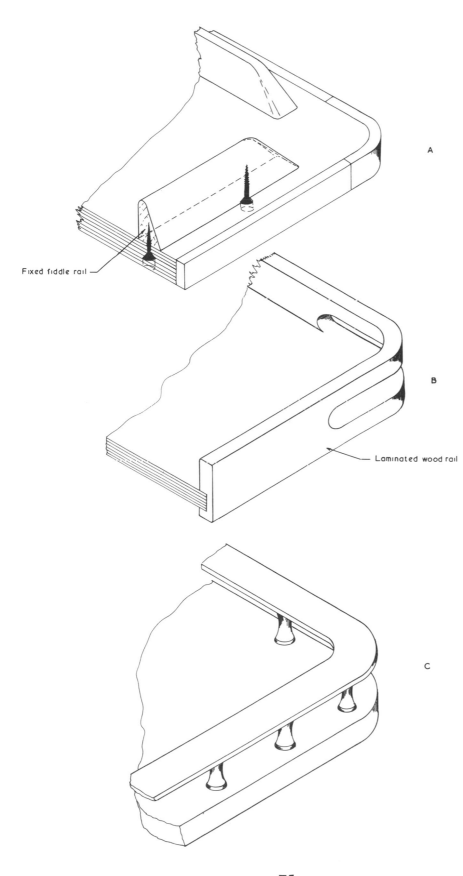

Fixed fiddle rail

Laminated wood rail

A

B

C

FIGURE 4

Corner details. In A the solid rail ends before the corner to leave an easy cleanout. In B the rail is molded around the corner, but a cutout is provided as both a handhold and a clean-out. In C the fiddle rail is taken completely around the corner, but the counter can still be cleaned under the rail.

F I G U R E   5

To make a removable rail, or sea rail, put wood screws in the bottom of the rail and cut their heads off. Drill corresponding holes in the table and insert short lengths of brass tube. The screws should fit into the brass tube.

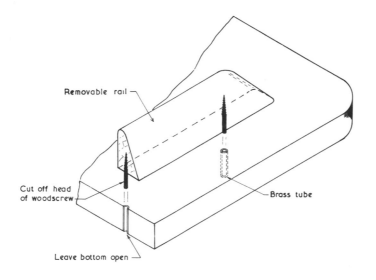

Removable rail

Cut off head of woodscrew

Brass tube

Leave bottom open

P R O J E C T 4 - 7
ADDING EXTRA DRAWERS

In the early days of yachting there used to be an adage that ran, "You can tell the quality of a boat by the number of drawers it has." Today this is still very true, because manufacturers save cost by eliminating drawers in favor of less-expensive lockers or shelves. Here we'll look at making drawers to fit in existing lockers or in place of shelves to give your boat a look of quality.

Figure 1 shows a space that was originally intended to be a locker. By trimming away more of the front of the lockers or fitting a new face, drawers can be added, as shown in Figure 2. Figure 3 shows sections through the drawers in both transverse and longitudinal directions.

In Figure 4 the drawer slides (S) are glued and screwed to the existing shelves. You could also remove the shelves and fit commercially available metal drawer slides. Note the wedge-shaped notches at the end of the slides. These keep the drawer in place when the boat is heeled (more about that later). The drawer is shown disassembled on the right of this picture. The grooves in the drawer sides are cut with a router or dadoed, and the sides and end pieces are glued

in place. You might want to use small finish nails to hold the pieces together while the glue is drying. The front of the drawer is a solid piece of wood with a recess routed out around the edges. The section in Figure 4A shows the detail. B is the bottom of the drawer, and A is the drawer front. The dashed line is a recess routed into the bottom of the drawer front as a finger pull. This will allow you to lift and pull the drawer out. A small wedge is fitted onto the side of the drawer as a stop.

Some drawer makers prefer to build a drawer with four plywood sides and to screw the front on later. Figure 4B gives a section showing how this is done. A is the plywood front of the drawer, and B is the drawer front. C is the base of the drawer.

Figure 5 shows the operating principle of the wedge. As the drawer is pushed in and closed, the wedge on the drawer slides over the lip and into the recess in the slide. This holds the drawer firmly closed when the boat is heeled. To open the drawer, the front is lifted and pulled. This lifts the wedge out of its recess, allowing the drawer to be pulled open.

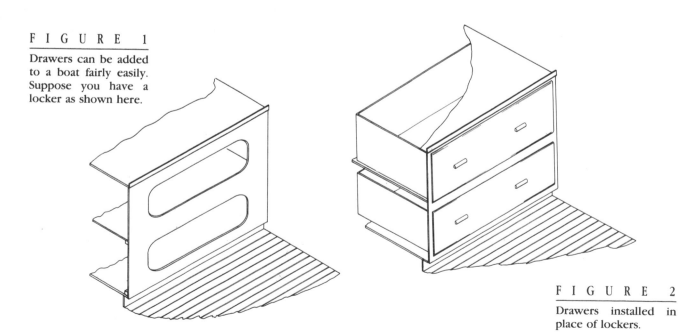

F I G U R E 1
Drawers can be added to a boat fairly easily. Suppose you have a locker as shown here.

F I G U R E 2
Drawers installed in place of lockers.

F I G U R E 3

If you want to convert to drawers as shown in Figure 2, the first step is to measure the space carefully. Make sure you have room to open the drawers fully and plenty of space for runners and supports.

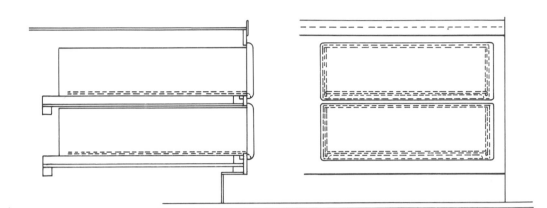

F I G U R E 4

In this figure the drawer will run on wooden slides (S). The edges of the drawer fit outside the slide. Note the wedge at the end. The drawer itself is assembled by cutting all four sides out and either dadoing with a table saw or routing a groove to make the bottom. Note how the groove is cut vertically to fit the end of the drawer.

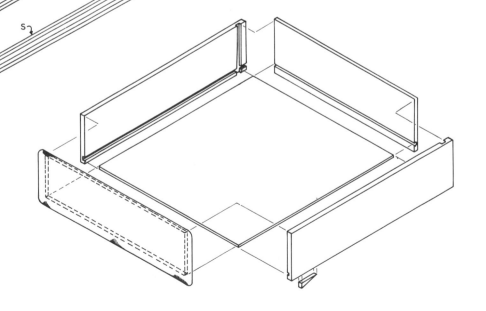

F I G U R E 4A

If the drawer front is made as part of the drawer structure, it should be fitted as shown here, with the bottom nailed and glued to the front face of the drawer. Note that the dashed line is cut out for a finger pull.

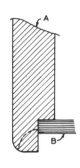

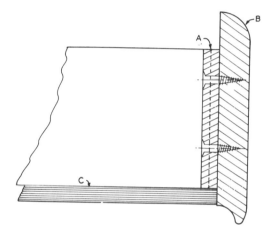

F I G U R E 4B

This sketch shows how drawer sides are assembled and then the front face is added later. The face is back-screwed through the front panel. This is the best way of making the drawer front if a varnished finish is to be used.

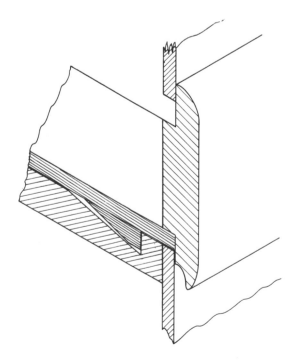

F I G U R E 5

Magnetic catches should not be used to hold a drawer closed. Here a wedge is fitted to the bottom of the drawer. When the drawer is opened it must be lifted until the wedge clears the runner.

PROJECT 4 - 8
DESIGNING AN ICEBOX

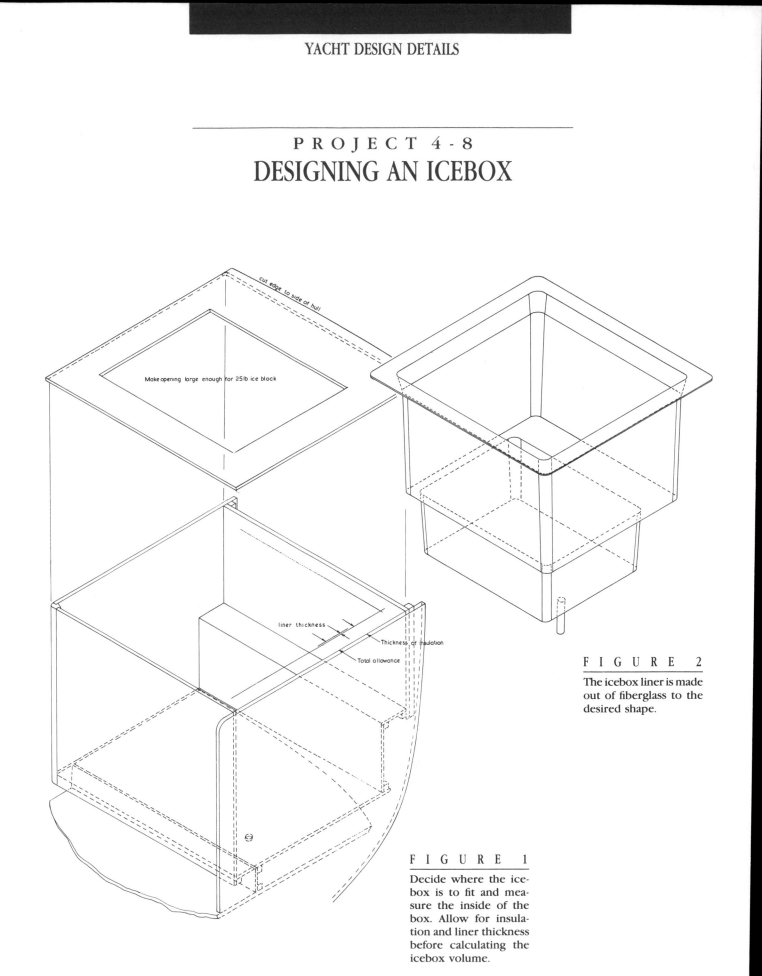

cut edge to side of hull

Make opening large enough for 25lb ice block

liner thickness

Thickness of insulation

Total allowance

F I G U R E   2

The icebox liner is made out of fiberglass to the desired shape.

F I G U R E   1

Decide where the icebox is to fit and measure the inside of the box. Allow for insulation and liner thickness before calculating the icebox volume.

Suppose you have a locker near the galley that is not really essential for stowing gear. You can convert that locker into an icebox with very little effort. First you need to figure out if you can add enough insulation and still have room for frozen food.

Figure 1 shows how an icebox is laid out. Begin by using cardboard to determine where the shelves and shelf supports will go. The box should have a flat bottom rather than be contoured to the shape of the hull, so it is usual to install the bottom above the level of the hull. This positioning of the bottom also allows you to reach the drain fittings and

install a kick space if desired. Having mocked up the exterior dimensions, allow for the thickness of the insulation—2 inches (50 mm) is minimum, 3 inches (75 mm) is better. Then add the liner thickness—usually ¼ inch (6 mm) is enough. If the interior of the box is still large enough, you can move on to the next stage, designing the liner.

Figure 2 shows the liner of the box in Figure 1. Note the drain hole and the lip around the inside of the shelf. An alternative layout is shown assembled in Figure 3, where the icebox is too small for a second shelf and no shelf lip is required.

FIGURE 3

A slightly different icebox. This one is simpler and easier to make and does not have any shelves inside.

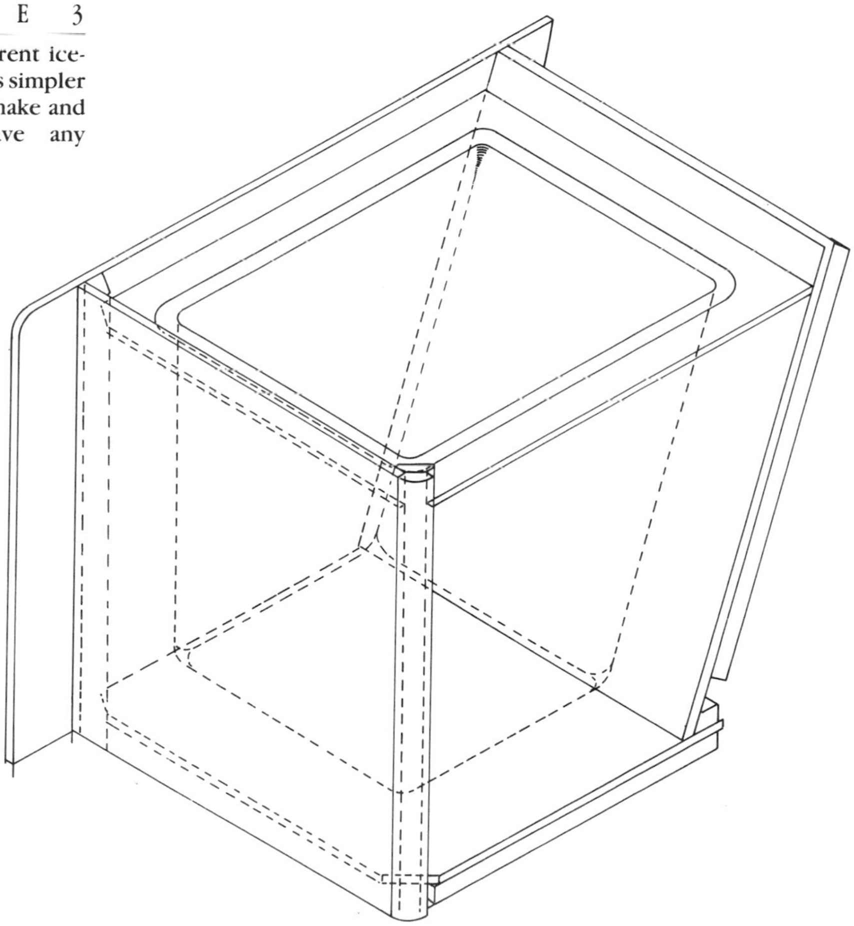

P R O J E C T   4 - 9
MAKING THE LINER, LID, AND SHELVES

To make the fiberglass liner for an icebox, you must first make a mold, as illustrated in Figure 1. Note that the edges of the laminate are stopped before the corner, and the corners are filled with putty or car-body filler to make a smooth rounded corner (Figure 1A). I like to make a large radius here so that food particles are easy to clean out of the corners. The drain is very simple. At this stage it can be a piece of pipe or dowel of the correct diameter, glued or bolted into place on the corner.

When the liner mold is made, it should be carefully smoothed. The smoother it is, the better the inside of your icebox will be. After smoothing, follow the manufacturer's instructions and apply mold-release wax and lay up the fiberglass (see page 15 for notes on using and laying up fiberglass around a mold). Three or four alternating layers of chop strand and woven roving should be sufficient. Allow the liner to cure, and pop it off the mold. (Most experts recommend at least 24 hours for fiberglass to cure, but you should allow 3 days or more to ensure that the liner has set up properly.) Clean up the edges (by trimming with a sharp saw or file), including around the drain, and it is ready to be installed.

Figures 2 and 2A show the various layers of exterior furniture or wooden box, vapor barrier, foam, and liner, that should be in the box. Once the exterior furniture has been built around the new icebox position, the entire unit should be lined with a vapor barrier. This is simply a plastic, Mylar, or metal foil to prevent condensation problems and cold air escaping. Try to use a heavy-grade (5 mil or better) plastic or Mylar to prevent tears and degradation during construction. On top of the vapor barrier, lay the foam. It can be cut approximately to size and the gaps filled with spray-in-place foam. Next drop in the liner. Hopefully, when all the foam is in it, it will still fit. Secure it by screwing through the flange into the wooden support around the rim.

The icebox lid is the next stage. It, too, needs a mold, but this one is much simpler. You will need two lids, and each can be made off the same mold. They should be made as shown in Figure 3 (Page 88). The voids behind the lid should have a vapor barrier and foam to prevent air escaping. Add trim pieces around the edge of the lid to finish it properly and rubber gaskets along the lower edges to stop air escaping from the box. Project 4–10 shows the details more clearly.

Figure 4 (Page 88) shows how a shelf, made of clear plastic laminate, can be fabricated. It drops in and sits on the lips illustrated in Figure 3. If you prefer, you can make a shelf grating according to the instructions given in Project 3–1.

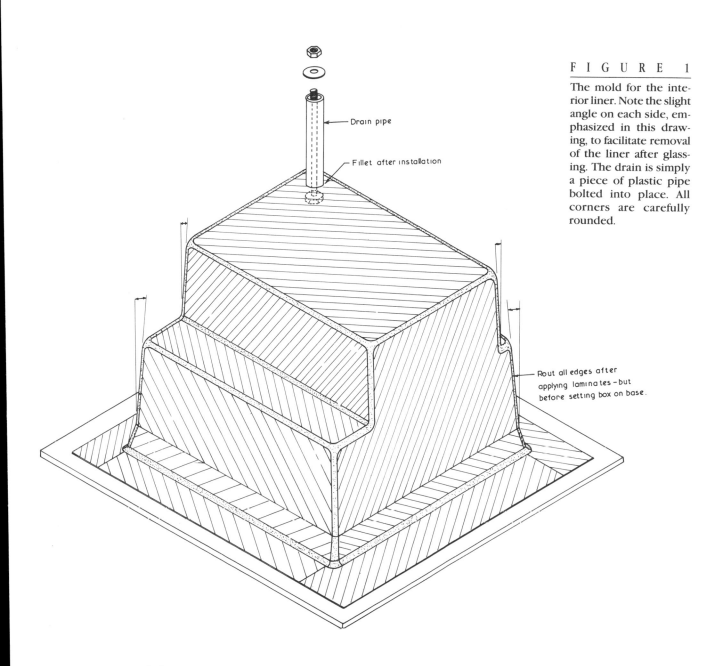

Drain pipe

Fillet after installation

Rout all edges after
applying laminates – but
before setting box on base.

The mold for the interior liner. Note the slight angle on each side, emphasized in this drawing, to facilitate removal of the liner after glassing. The drain is simply a piece of plastic pipe bolted into place. All corners are carefully rounded.

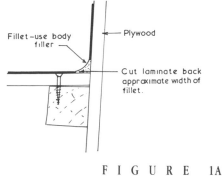

Fillet–use body
filler

Plywood

Cut laminate back
approximate width of
fillet.

F I G U R E 1A
Corner detail showing how the fillet is installed.

83

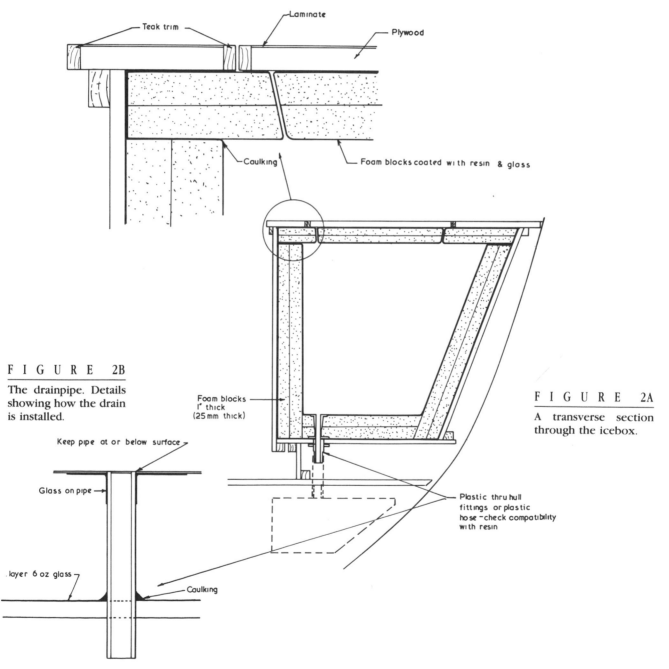

F I G U R E   2

A transverse section through the icebox showing construction details.

Teak trim

Laminate

Plywood

Caulking

Foam blocks coated with resin & glass

F I G U R E   2B

The drainpipe. Details showing how the drain is installed.

Foam blocks 1" thick (25 mm thick)

Keep pipe at or below surface

Glass on pipe

layer 6 oz glass

Caulking

F I G U R E   2A

A transverse section through the icebox.

Plastic thru hull fittings or plastic hose – check compatibility with resin

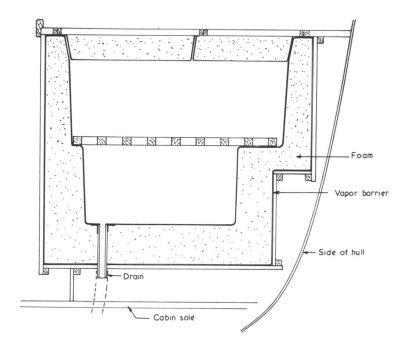

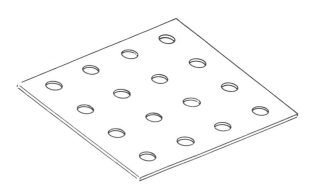

F I G U R E   3

A longitudinal section through the same box.

Foam

Vapor barrier

Side of hull

Drain

Cabin sole

F I G U R E   4

A grating for the icebox can be made as shown in Project 3-1. Or the shelf can be made from translucent plastic with some 1-inch (25-mm) holes drilled in it.

FITTING THE ICEBOX

Figure 1 (opposite) and Figure 2A (page 84) show sections through an inexpensively constructed icebox. In Figure 1 the foam insulation is cut out of flat sheets of construction foam. While this is not ideal, it will work. The layers are glued together, and all voids are filled with spray-in-place foam from an aerosol can. The liner is the simple model illustrated as Figure 2 in Project 4–8. A wooden grating shelf is fitted and located on alloy brackets screwed into the side of the box; Figure 1A shows the details. If you make a small lip in the edge of the icebox, the grating should be large enough to fit comfortably on the lip, as shown in Figure 2.

The drain is a simple plastic pipe glassed in place as shown in Figure 2B (Page 84). Note how caulking is applied to prevent water getting behind the vapor barrier. Figure 2A (Page 84) shows a slightly different type of drain fitting. This uses plastic through-hull fittings that fit into each other to provide a leakproof seal. Both drains empty into a sump tank. Do not drain the icebox into the bilge. The discharge will eventually smell and require major bilge washing to prevent smelling out the whole boat. If you don't want to go to the expense of purchasing a metal or glass tank, a simple bladder tank will suffice.

The lid of this icebox is made of fiberglass, shaped as shown in Figure 3. Note that the edges next to the hinge have their flanges reversed. This must be done after the lid is removed from the mold. It is done to enable the hinge to be screwed in place and to provide a place that can be glued or screwed to the wooden part of the lid. Figure 1B shows the hinge laid out. Note the blocking and reversed flanges.

When fitting the lid to the box, make sure the edges fit snugly and install a rubber gasket all around the top, as shown in Figure 1C. Figure 4 shows a slightly different method whereby the countertop is trimmed up carefully and the foam sloped to provide a positive landing place for the lid. But even here the rubber gasket is essential.

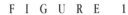

F I G U R E   1

A longitudinal section through the simple icebox shown in Figure 3 of drawing 4-10. In this box the shelf is held in place with a piece of nonferrous-metal angle.

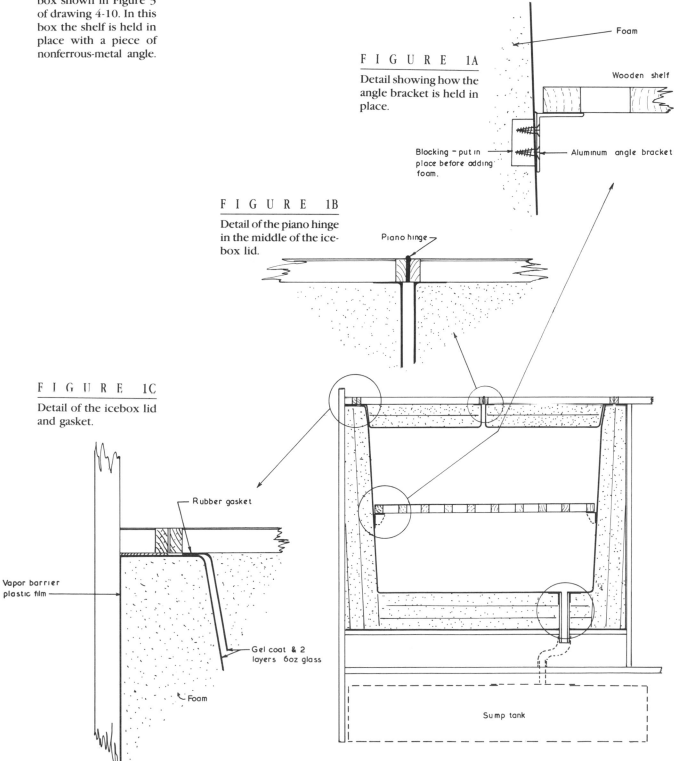

F I G U R E   1A

Detail showing how the angle bracket is held in place.

Foam

Wooden shelf

Blocking – put in place before adding foam.

Aluminum angle bracket

F I G U R E   1B

Detail of the piano hinge in the middle of the icebox lid.

Piano hinge

F I G U R E   1C

Detail of the icebox lid and gasket.

Rubber gasket

Vapor barrier plastic film

Gel coat & 2 layers 6oz glass

Foam

Sump tank

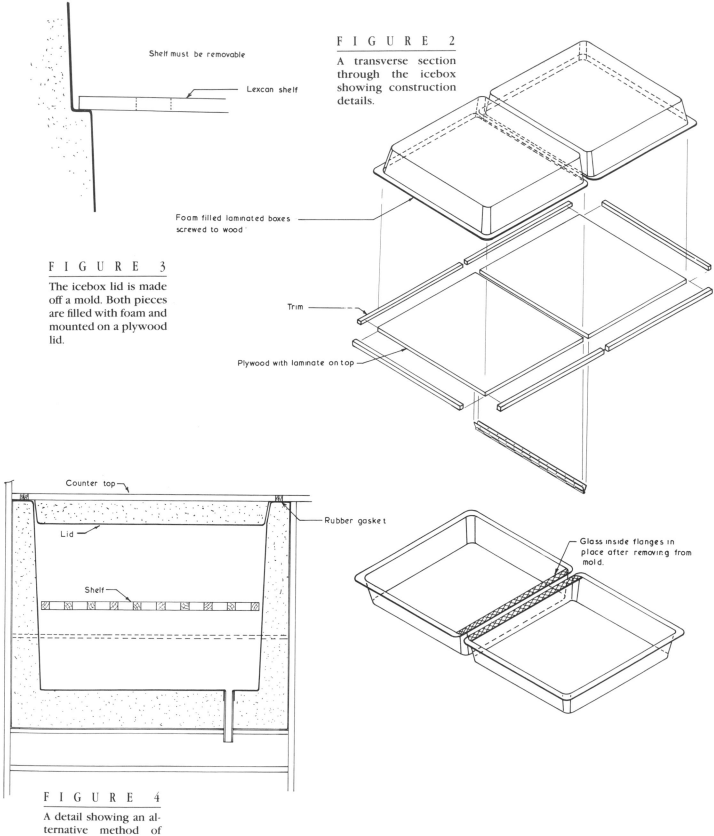

Shelf must be removable

Lexcan shelf

FIGURE 2
A transverse section through the icebox showing construction details.

Foam filled laminated boxes screwed to wood

FIGURE 3
The icebox lid is made off a mold. Both pieces are filled with foam and mounted on a plywood lid.

Trim

Plywood with laminate on top

Counter top

Rubber gasket

Lid

Glass inside flanges in place after removing from mold.

Shelf

FIGURE 4
A detail showing an alternative method of supporting the icebox lid.

PROJECT 4 - 11
FITTING LEEBOARDS

How many times have you turned in on an offshore cruise and found that the leeboard was too low or couldn't be adjusted properly? Very few production builders install leeboards on their boats, so it is up to the owner to fit them. There are various types, both wooden and cloth, that can be fixed to bunks.

Figure 1 shows a wooden leeboard. When not in use, it is folded under the mattress. Note that the leeboard in Figure 1A is tapered to eliminate a bump in the mattress and that it has two positions. The vertical position is used in inclement weather, when you should be snugged in tightly, and the open position is used in moderate or hot weather, when more room is required.

Figure 2 shows a leecloth. This one is attached at the outboard edge of the bunk. As long as the bunk edge is low,

this is a perfectly acceptable method of securing the leecloth. However, if the side of the bunk is fairly high, it can be quite uncomfortable for the occupant. Figure 2A shows how the bunk side would dig into the occupant when the boat is heeled. This problem can be eliminated by putting the leecloth on the outboard side of the bunk, as shown in Figure 3. The cloth is tightened sufficiently to raise the occupant above the edge of the bunk. This also raises the cushion and can be quite comfortable when the boat is heeled.

Note also how the leecloth is secured to the overhead rail or pad eye as shown in Figure 3A. Both the rail and pad eye should be through-bolted for maximum security. The line from the leecloth should be tied with a slipknot to allow the occupant to get out of the bunk fast if an emergency should occur.

F I G U R E 1

A wooden leeboard can be made adjustable to give the occupant more room in favorable conditions.

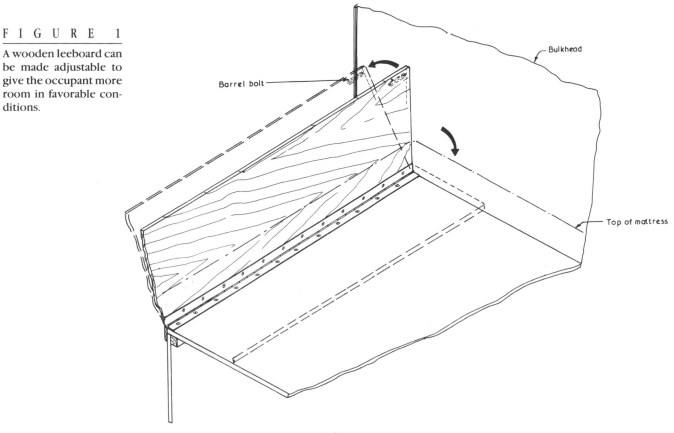

Barrel bolt

Bulkhead

Top of mattress

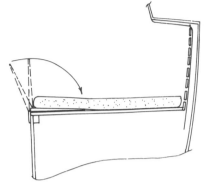

F I G U R E   1A

A section through the bunk shows the tapered leeboard and how it can be adjusted.

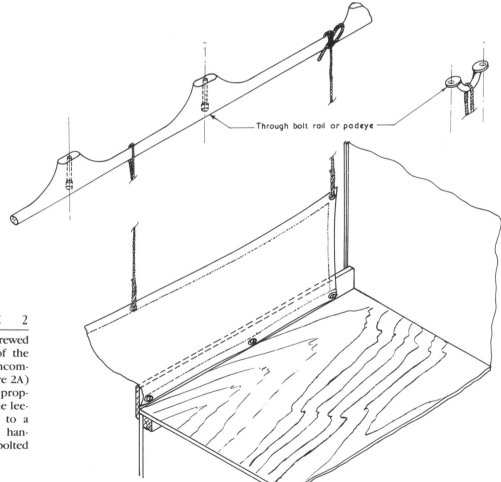

Through bolt rail or padeye

F I G U R E   2

A cloth leeboard screwed to the outside of the berth can be uncomfortable (see Figure 2A) if not installed properly. Note how the leecloth is secured to a strongly fastened handrail or a through-bolted pad eye.

FIGURE 2A

The section through this bunk shows how the coaming distorts the shape of the leecloth, making the bunk un-comfortable.

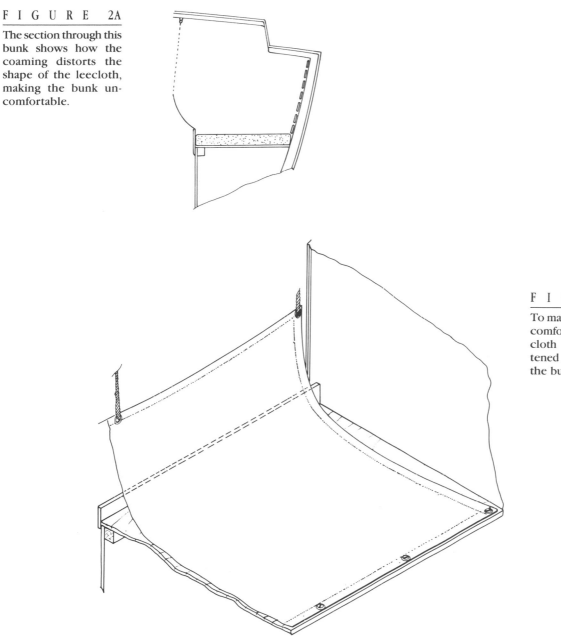

FIGURE 3

To make the bunk really comfortable, the lee-cloth should be fas-tened to the inside of the bunk.

FIGURE 3A

A section through the bunk shows how the leecloth can be used to raise the mattress for more comfortable sleeping. Tightening the leecloth even more can compensate for heel when the boat is under sail.

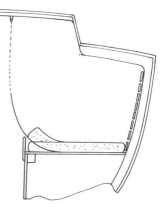

91

P R O J E C T   4 - 12
ADDING AN EXTRA BERTH

If you are like many sailors, you have at sometime slept on sailbags when there haven't been enough berths. Here's a simple emergency berth that can be installed behind an existing seat back so that it is ready should an extra guest be aboard.

Figure 1 shows the canvas berth (dashed lines) hidden behind a seat back. When needed, it folds out, as shown in Figure 2. The berth is made from two alloy pipes about 1½ inches (37 mm) diameter, cut to the correct length, and a canvas bunk bottom. The canvas is fastened to the pipe on the inboard side by the method shown in *A* or *B*. If you want to remove the canvas for cleaning, you need not fasten the canvas on the inboard side. But it is more secure when it is fastened on both sides. A wooden fitting holds the pipes on the bulkhead. The wooden pieces at *X* and *Y* hold the bunk flat against the side of the boat when not in use. When you need to use the bunk, simply lift out the outer tube and place it in the fittings at *V* and *Z*. The three different levels are for sailing on different tacks. These will be effective only if there is enough room for both bunks to be used.

A variation on this is to make the bottom bunk a canvas one as well. In this way, the lower occupant has more room because he will be lower in the bunk. But now the lower level is too low to be used as a seat. It requires an adjustment to make it tight enough. Figure 3 shows a section through the bunks. The lower bunk is used as a seat in the *T* position, as a bunk in the *N* position, or, in heavier weather, it can be lowered to the *S* position to keep the occupant safe. The adjustment is achieved by rolling one side of the bunk up. Figure 3A shows the bunk unrolled, and 3B shows it rolled. The actual method of rolling is shown in Figures 4 and 4A. In Figure 4 a circular wooden block is fastened to the pipe. The canvas (also fastened to the pipe) is rolled up, and a pin is inserted through the block into the bulkhead fitting at *V* and *Z*. An option is to make the block square, as shown in Figure 4A, and drop it into the square hole. This requires identical square U-shaped blocks at *V* and *Z*.

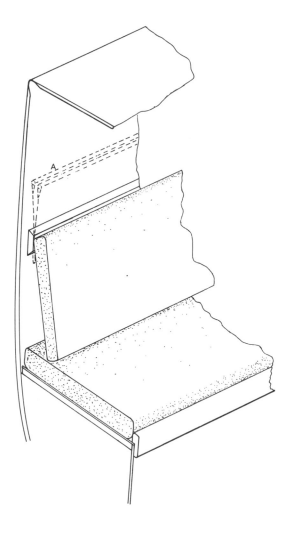

F I G U R E   1

A simple canvas bunk will fold down behind an existing seat back.

F I G U R E   2

When in use, the outboard side of the canvas bunk is simply fitted into the specially made wooden holders at X and Y. The inboard side fits into the holders at Z and V. Note the different levels, which enable the occupant to compensate for heel angle. The canvas is fastened to the pipes by either looping it over the pipe and fastening with sheet metal screws and grommets or folding it around a metal bar about ½ inch by ⅛ inch (12 mm × 3 mm) and screwing that to the pipe. The methods are shown in details A and B.

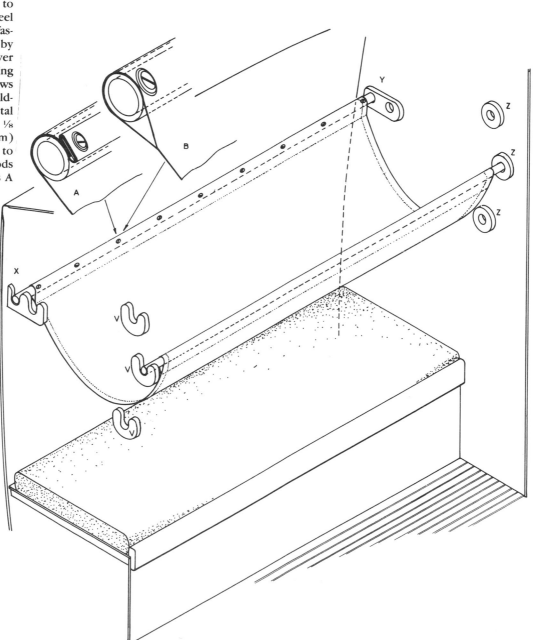

FIGURE 3

A variation on this idea is to make the inboard pipe rotate. In the section shown, turning the pipe so that it is fully wound makes the canvas tight as at T. The normal sitting position is at N, but if the weather is very bad and you want to be totally secure, you can use the deep position at S.

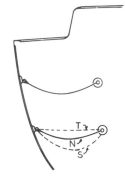

FIGURE 3A

If the canvas is sewn as shown here, it will be easy to slide onto the pipe and can then be fastened with a grommet and screw to make it easy to roll.

FIGURE 3B

The canvas bunk is rolled to tension it by simply turning the pipe.

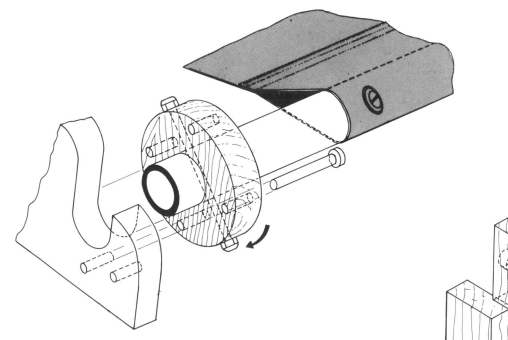

FIGURE 4

To hold the pipe when the canvas is tight, a special round block is bolted onto the end of the pipe. When the bunk is wound up, the pin is inserted through the block into the fitting on the bulkhead.

FIGURE 4A

Another method with slightly less finesse is to make the block on the pipe square. It is dropped into the square slot on the bulkhead-mounted block.

PROJECT 4 - 13

ADDING SHELVES
AND STORAGE SPACES

There are many places on a boat that could benefit from a small shelf or drop-down table. For instance, a fold-away table, as shown in Figure 5, next to a bunk will provide a handy place to put your book or nightcap when the boat is anchored in a quiet harbor. A tray as shown in Figure 7 makes it easier to pour hot or cold drinks when the boat is beating into a head sea. This set of drawings, then, adds some of the features that help to make sailing comfortable, but are not often seen on today's production boats.

Figure 1 shows the basics of a simple shelf. A support or cleat on either side, screwed or glued to the bulkhead or locker side, and a flat, usually plywood shelf, screwed down on top of them. Across the front is a low fiddle to stop small objects from sliding off.

Figure 2 shows how a set of shelves can be installed in a convenient space. By spacing the shelves evenly, they can be used for many purposes: lockers, bookshelves, and so forth. To stop everything falling off the shelves when the boat heels, you can add a locker front, as shown in Figure 3. This is simply two vertical braces or cleats to which a piece of plywood is fastened. The plywood is cut out and removed in way of the doors. The doors are mounted on hinges and open outward.

Figure 4 shows a collapsible shelf. If the two supports are folded under, the top of the shelf can fold down against the locker side. This is ideal for a position where extra counter-space is required for short periods of time, such as in the galley or toilet compartment.

Section through shelf

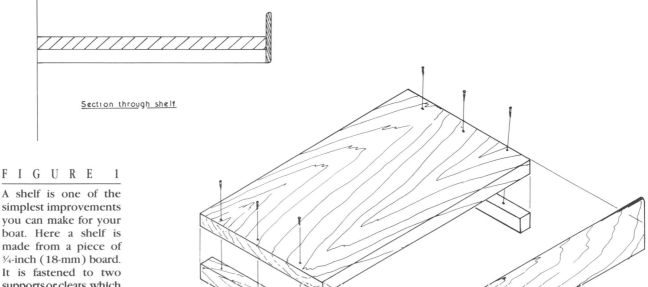

FIGURE 1

A shelf is one of the simplest improvements you can make for your boat. Here a shelf is made from a piece of ¾-inch (18-mm) board. It is fastened to two supports or cleats, which are themselves screwed to a bulkhead or locker side. On the front of the shelf is a fiddle to stop items from falling off when the boat heels.

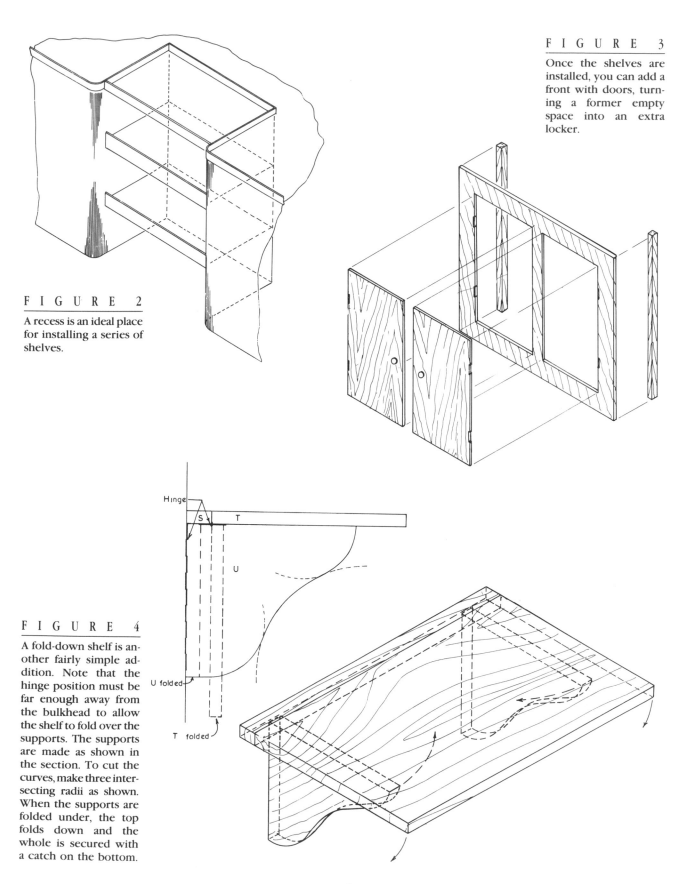

FIGURE 2

A recess is an ideal place for installing a series of shelves.

FIGURE 3

Once the shelves are installed, you can add a front with doors, turning a former empty space into an extra locker.

FIGURE 4

A fold-down shelf is another fairly simple addition. Note that the hinge position must be far enough away from the bulkhead to allow the shelf to fold over the supports. The supports are made as shown in the section. To cut the curves, make three intersecting radii as shown. When the supports are folded under, the top folds down and the whole is secured with a catch on the bottom.

The shelf shown in Figure 5 works on the same principle but has only one support. This may be used alongside a bunk to provide a space for your book or coffee cup. On both of these shelves measurements must be precise. Part *S* should be at least as thick as the support (part *U*) to ensure that the top (*T*) can fold down flat against the support.

In Figure 6 a wooden sink cover is shown. It should be made to fit snugly into the sink. Figure 6A shows two examples of the edge detail. In *X* the edge of the shelf is routed to form a lip that supports the cover on the edge of the sink. In *Y* a wire frame passes under the cover from side to side. The wire sits on the edge of the sink and supports the cover.

Often when you are at sea, it is difficult to pour hot drinks for the crew. You either end up spilling liquid everywhere or filling the cups less than half full. By making this rack to fit over the stove, you can take advantage of the gimballed action of the stove to keep cups horizontal. Once the cups are filled, the rack can be used as a tray to carry the drinks on deck or to the table. The rack is made from four pieces of wood, the top and bottom and two side pieces. The top and bottom can be ¼-inch (6 mm) plywood, while the side pieces should be 1½-inch by 1-inch (37 mm × 25 mm) lumber. Cut the top piece as shown to fit the cups and glue it to the side pieces. Then glue and screw the bottom in place. Note the handholds at either end to make lifting the rack easy.

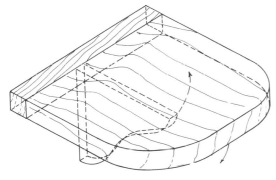

FIGURE 5

A variation on figure 4. This shelf has only one support arm and can be placed almost anywhere on the boat. You can install it as a bunkside shelf, an additional galley shelf, or in the head as an additional shelf for essentials.

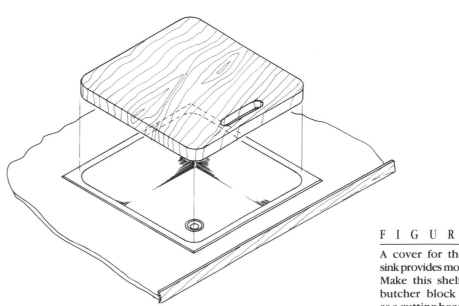

FIGURE 6

A cover for the galley sink provides more space. Make this shelf out of butcher block for use as a cutting board in the galley.

F I G U R E   6A

The edge detail of the shelf in Figure 6. Either rout the edge, as in X, so that the board will sit comfortably in the sink, or use a form metal wire fastened to the underside of the board to hold it in place. Another idea is to cut a hand hole in the board. This makes it easier to sweep peelings or cuttings through the hand hole into the sink for later disposal.

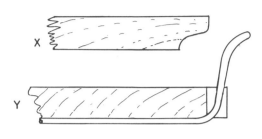

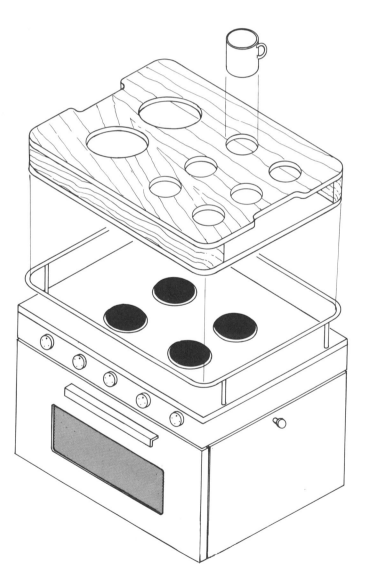

F I G U R E   7

The galley stove is another useful place when it is not in use. With two pieces of plywood and two supports, a lightweight rack can be made that fits easily into the space on top of the stove. If you cut holes in the top piece for cups, mugs, and pots and place the whole unit on the stove, you'll find they will stay put. In rough weather when the boat is heeled and bouncing around, the tray will stay on the gimballed stove while you pour soup or coffee.

P R O J E C T 4 - 14
MAKING PAPER-TOWEL, TOILET-ROLL, AND TOOTHBRUSH HOLDERS

On a yacht where the joiner work is teak or another attractive wood, a matching set of bathroom accessories can greatly enhance your enjoyment of the boat. In the following pages we'll look at making various holders for the toilet compartment and galley. Note that the style of the paper-towel holder can be adapted for towel racks, curtain rods, hanger rails in lockers, and even as a rack for sail ties in the forepeak or a suitable locker.

Figure 1 shows sections through the paper-towel holder. You will need to make two end pieces, a backing piece, and a dowel. Most paper-towel rolls are 11 inches (280 mm) long and about 4 inches (100 mm) in diameter. You should allow about ¼ inch (6 mm) at each end, making the distance between the inside faces of the end pieces 11½ inches (292 mm). Assembly of the unit is done as shown in Figure 1A. Note the holes for screwing it to the bulkhead. To fasten the end pieces to the back, use three screws, as shown in Figure 1B. Remember, if you use teak, it may be hard to glue, and you will probably want to screw it in place. Note also the groove in one end to accept the dowel. At the other end (not shown) a blind hole should be drilled just large enough to hold the dowel.

The toilet-roll holder shown in Figure 2 is made in exactly the same manner. Most toilet rolls are about 4½ inches (115 mm) in diameter. Allow an extra ¼ inch (6 mm) on each end and assemble the unit as outlined in Figure 1.

Using the same style of end pieces, you can make a curtain rack for the shower. Make the rack any length and screw the end pieces to a backing plate or directly to the bulkhead. The curtain—it can be a shower curtain or compartment divider—can be threaded onto the dowel and placed in the holders.

The principle is the same if you are making a sail tie holder or a towel rack. Make end pieces and screw them to a backing plate or directly to the bulkhead.

If you have a few pieces of teak left over, you may want to make a soap dish, as shown in Figure 3. The backing piece is simply a block with four holes drilled in it. The holes are used to screw the holder to the bulkhead. The dish itself is slightly more complex in that it has a hollow routed into it to hold the soap. A small hole is then drilled in the middle of the dish to allow water to drain off the soap. It is secured to the backing plate with three screws, in the same manner as shown in Figure 1B. Figure 3A shows the assembled unit.

Another item that will add charm to your toilet fixtures is a glass and toothbrush holder as shown in Figure 4. Make sure the hole for the glass is the right size to fit the particular glass you intend to use. The holes for toothbrushes should be about ¼ inch by ½ inch (6 mm × 12 mm) with rounded ends. The layout is shown in Figure 4 and the assembled unit in Figure 4A. You should carefully round off or miter any corners to eliminate sharp edges.

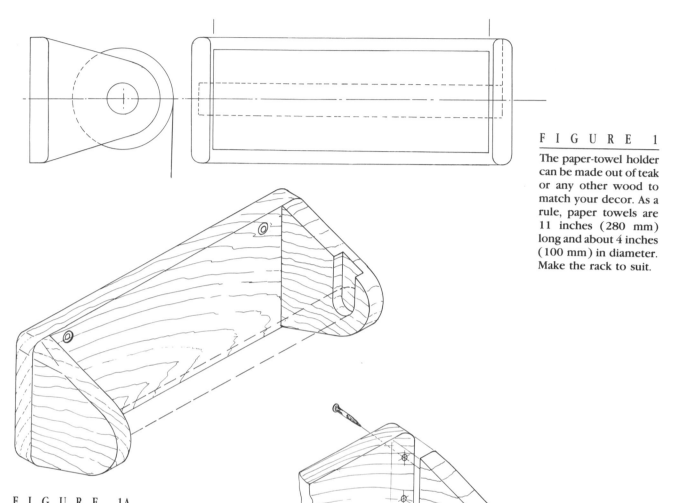

F I G U R E   1

The paper-towel holder can be made out of teak or any other wood to match your decor. As a rule, paper towels are 11 inches (280 mm) long and about 4 inches (100 mm) in diameter. Make the rack to suit.

F I G U R E   1A

The towel holder, showing how it is assembled. Cut a groove in one end for the towel rod and drill a hole halfway into the other end for the other end of the rod. Use a 1½-inch (37-mm) piece of dowel as the

towel holder. If you wish to make a matching towel rack for the head, use the same style end pieces and fasten them directly to the bulkhead. In this case drill both ends halfway through to make the dowel captive.

F I G U R E   1B

Shows how to join the end fitting to the backing piece. Use three brass or bronze screws. If you are joining teak, you may have a hard job gluing it; other woods glue more easily.

F I G U R E   2

The toilet-roll holder is similar to the paper-towel holder except that it is shorter. In general, toilet rolls are about 4½ inches (115 mm) wide. Make the ends in the same manner and fasten to the backing piece using three screws as outlined in Figure 1B.

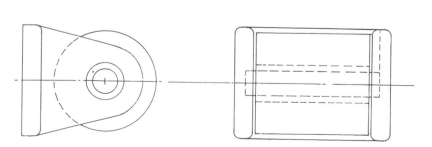

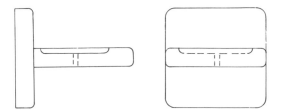

F I G U R E   3

A soap dish is another piece of bathroom hardware that can be fabricated from a few pieces of scrap teak. Make it 4 inches square and remember to drill a hole in the bottom to allow the soap to drain.

F I G U R E   3A

The soap dish holder is reasonably easy to make.

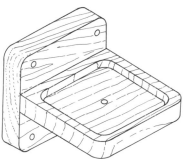

F I G U R E   4

Another item to make the matching set is a glass and toothbrush holder. This drawing shows how the holder is laid out. Make sure you select the glass before cutting a hole in the wood.

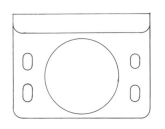

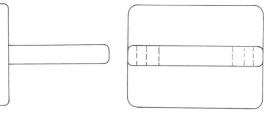

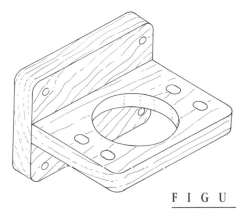

F I G U R E   4A

The glass and toothbrush holder assembled.

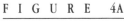

P R O J E C T   4 - 15
MAKING A MEDICINE CABINET
OR SPICE RACK

In the previous drawing we saw most of the toilet fixtures. Here we'll add a mirror and a medicine cabinet. The construction principles are the same for a galley spice rack or bookshelves, so we'll also look at how they are made.

Figure 1 shows the method of making the mirror. It is simply a molding, cut and mitered at each corner. This will give you four mitered side pieces. Next comes the mirror—I would recommend a Mylar-coated mirror rather than a glass one, and a backing piece of ⅛-inch (3 mm) or ¼-inch (6 mm) plywood the same size as the mirror.

To assemble the unit, glue the side pieces, top and bottom, together to form a square frame—make sure they are set up squarely. When the glue is dry, place the mirror and the backing plywood in the frame and glue the frame and the backing plywood together at the edges. Use framing brads to hold the mirror and plywood in place while the glue around the edge of the plywood dries.

To mount the mirror on the bulkhead, screw small mounting brackets to the edges of the side frames and then screw them to the bulkhead. Do not hang on a string or wire frame for use on the boat. If you intend using the mirror as the door to the medicine cabinet, then some small hinges and a catch—preferably nonmagnetic—should be mounted on the backside of the unit.

To make the spice rack, book storage, or medicine cabinet you will need to measure the size carefully and cut out the parts shown in Figure 3. There are three shelves shown, all of which are the same size, but you can make any number of shelves in your rack. They fit into grooves routed or dadoed into the side pieces. Remember to cut a groove around the back of the unit for the back to be fitted into. The small crossbars are to hold items in the cabinet or books in the bookshelf when the boat heels. Figure 2 shows a slightly different example of a spice rack or bookshelf fully assembled.

To finish the medicine cabinet cut a slot for the hinges on one of the vertical supports and mount the hinges. The cabinet should be finished with varnish or paint and mounted on the bulkhead in the head compartment. Use hanging brackets at the top and bottom to mount the cabinet; do not screw through the back.

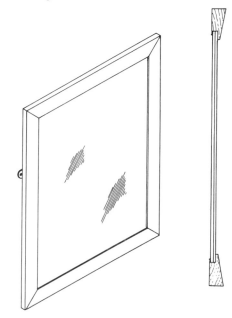

F I G U R E   1

The first step is to make the mirrored door. If you want to, you can forget about the rest of the cabinet and simply mount the mirror directly onto the bulkhead. Obtain a mirror cut to about 24 inches by 18 inches (610 mm × 460 mm). It can be larger or smaller to fit the space available. Cut a piece of ¼-inch (6-mm) plywood to the same size and put it behind the mirror. Now cut the frame and glue it together. When the glue is dry, the mirror and backing piece can be installed using picture-framing brads. You might want to glue the plywood backing to the frame if the mirror is to be used as the door to the medicine cabinet.

FIGURE 2

This figure shows the spice rack assembled. Note the bars across the front to keep the spice jars in place. Make the height of the rack to suit your favorite spice jars or cans.

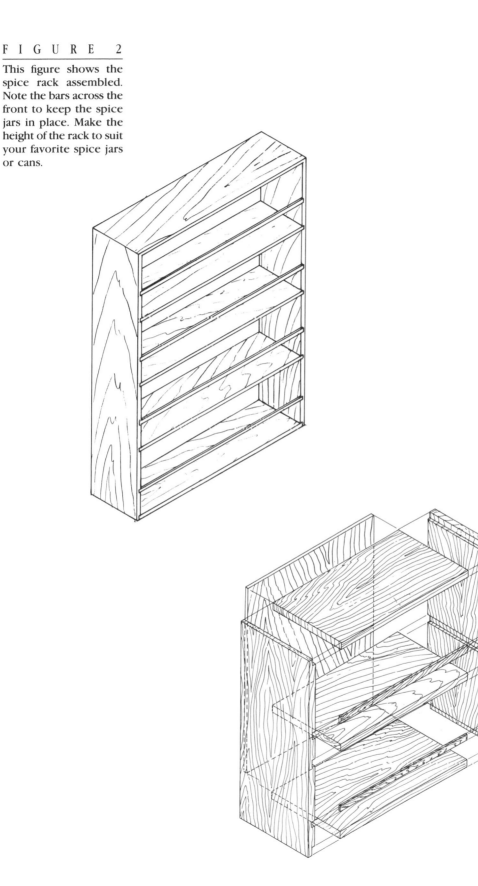

FIGURE 3

An exploded view of the medicine cabinet or spice rack. The shelves are fitted into routed grooves on the support pieces. Note that the backing piece fits into a groove around the perimeter of the back of the cabinet (not shown). The bars across the front should be installed in both the medicine cabinet and the spice rack to stop items from falling out when the door is opened. When the back is made, the mirrored door can be mounted on the front, making a unit that matches the towel, brush, and soap holder in the previous section.

P R O J E C T   4 - 16
ADDING AN EXTRA BUNK

Figure 1 shows a typical bunk/settee arrangement that you might find on a modern cruising boat. The upper bunk is outboard with lockers under it, while the lower is also used as a settee. To convert this to a double-bunk arrangement, you can do several things. Figure 2 shows how the seat back can be reinforced with a piece of plywood and laid on supports glued and screwed to the bulkheads. Figure 2A shows a section through this bunk arrangement. The supports will be visible at all times, so you should try to get wood that matches the bulkhead.

Figure 3 has a different arrangement. Here a separate extension transom is built into the existing bunk. The transom arms slide under the lockers when not in use. This is indicated by the section in Figure 3A. When the bunk is to be used as a double, the extension is pulled out, where it rests on two small supports at either end as shown in B. If

the bulkhead is not close enough to mount the supports on, you may have to make drop-down legs that fold away under the bunk when not in use.

Figure 4 shows another variation. Here the bunk flat is hinged along the front. To turn the bunk into a double, the cushions should be removed and the bunk opened. Figure 4A shows a section through this bunk. Figure 5 shows yet another method of obtaining more bunk space. Here the lockers have been removed and a double made by removing the seat back and laying on supports outside the settee in a method similar to that shown in Figure 2. The space that was formerly occupied by the lockers becomes available for sleeping. Note also that the space can still be used as a locker when the seat back is in place. It will hide any items stored behind it. Fasten the seat back in place with Velcro or small hooks and eyes.

F I G U R E   1

If you have a settee bunk set up like this, it might be helpful to change it into a double bunk.

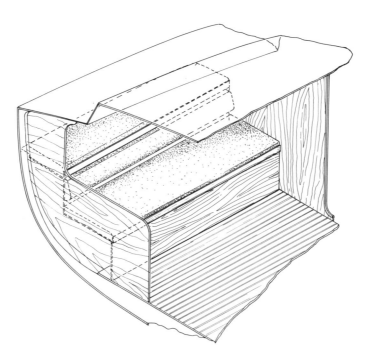

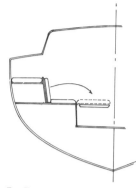

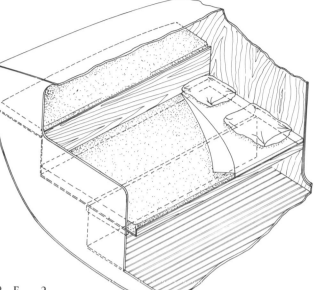

F I G U R E   2A

A section through the bunk arrangement. Note the supports will be glued and screwed to the bulkhead and should be made from a wood that closely matches the grain of the bulkhead.

F I G U R E   2

By adding supports to the bulkheads at either end of the bunk and mounting the seat cushion on a plywood board, extra space can be obtained.

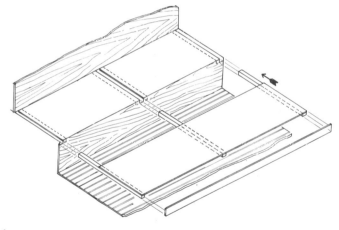

F I G U R E   3

A more complex method of converting to a double is to add a slide-away leaf as shown here. Grooves are cut in the existing bunk and supports added on either side. Then the extra piece is made. It has supports screwed to the underside. These slide into the grooves cut in the original bunk. When the bunk is needed, the extension is simply pulled out and rests on small supports screwed to the bulkhead. If there is no handy bulkhead, a hinge-down leg is a simple solution.

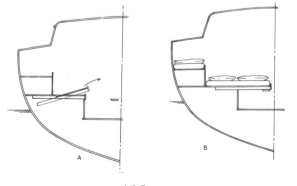

F I G U R E   3A

A section through the bunk described above, showing in A, how the extension is pulled out, and in B, how the bunk is made up using the settee back as an additional mattress.

F I G U R E   4

A slightly different variation of the double berth. In this example the berth is hinged along the front and folds out for use. It too can rest on supports screwed or bolted to the bulkhead or on legs that are hinged to the underside of the extension.

F I G U R E   4A

A section through the bunk shown in Figure 4.

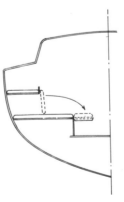

F I G U R E   5

Here the seat back is used as an extension berth. It is removed from in front of the lockers and placed on supports. If the lockers are removed entirely, a double berth can be made by utilizing the space under the upper berth. When the seat back is in its normal place (against the upper bunk), the space behind it can be used to stow gear.

PROJECT 4-17
IMPROVING THE WET LOCKER

All too often the wet locker is a collection of small cubbyholes that require you to roll up your foul-weather gear to stow it. If your gear is wet, it will never dry in such an environment. In Figure 1 a wet locker has been laid out that does almost everything. Foul-weather gear is hung on hangers to dry, thus spreading it out as far as possible. The base of the locker is a grating that allows the water to drain away into the bilge, where it can be pumped overside. On the side of the locker are Velcro straps for hanging towels, gloves, scarves, and other small items. The bottom of the locker has sturdy dowels—about 1 inch (25 mm) thick—on which boots are placed to dry.

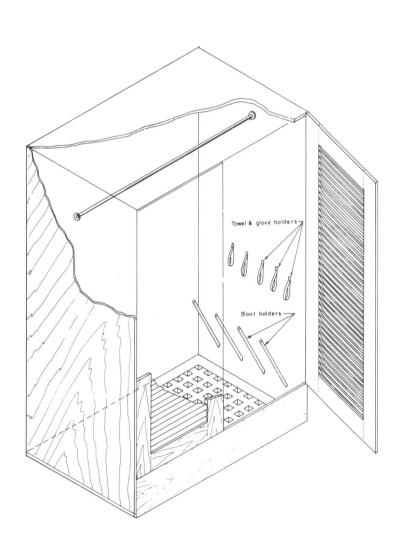

Towel & glove holders

Boot holders

F I G U R E 1

The ideal wet locker should have space for foul-weather gear, boots, gloves, scarves, harnesses, and life jackets. The locker illustrated here has that. Foul-weather gear is hung on wooden coat hangers to give it plenty of room to dry. Boots are dropped over the pegs in the bottom of the locker, while gloves, scarves, towels, and harnesses can be hung on the Velcro loops fastened to the side of the locker. Note the grating in the bottom of the locker to allow water to drain into the bilge.

Figure 3 shows how a boot fits over the dowels. The one drawback of this system is that water in the shoe or boot will collect in the toe. However, Figure 2 shows a different option. This one requires a slightly deeper locker. A false floor is fitted with holes cut in it for boots. Boots are simply dropped in the holes and allowed to drain. If you only have a few pairs of boots, you can make the rest of the space under the false floor into a locker for harnesses and lifejackets, keeping all the essential items in one place.

In locating the wet locker, if you have a choice, the ideal situation is somewhere near the engine, where the heat from the motor will help dry the wet gear. However, if you have to put the locker directly over the engine, make sure the grating drains into a pan that drains into the bilge. It is not good practice to allow wet gear to drain directly onto the engine. Not only can it ruin any electronics, it may also allow fumes and noise to escape into the cabin.

FIGURE 2

A boot turned upside down on a peg may hold water in the toes. Another option is to make a false bottom in the wet locker with holes for boots. But remember, shoes will fall through the holes. Depending on the number of crew, you may want to make the remaining area into a locker for lifejackets and harnesses.

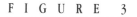

Round off end

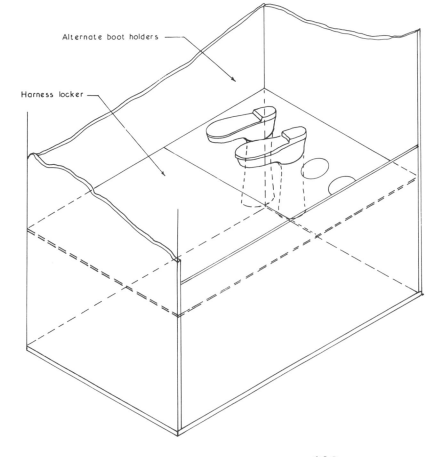

Alternate boot holders

Harness locker

FIGURE 3

Boots stowed on posts will hang downward, and water can collect in the toe. For this reason the locker with holes for boots may be better. Remember to round off the end of the post in order to eliminate damage.

HATCHES

No matter whether you sail on a day sailer or an offshore cruiser, there are few boats that do not have a hatch of some kind. Hatches vary tremendously in size and style. Aboard a small cruiser you may find a 6-inch-square (150 mm) hatch built into a sail tie locker and a foredeck hatch measuring several square feet. Despite the great difference between them, both do the job. In the following pages we'll look at several hatches, showing how to make and install them. Then we'll look at some of the options that can easily be built in.

A SIMPLE COMPANIONWAY HATCH

Fortunately, most boats come equipped with a companionway hatch. However, if you are refitting a hatch or building a new boat, it helps to know how to put one together. Project 5-1 shows one of the simplest of companionway hatches. Figure 1 is a companionway hatch made of two runners with a clear laminate or plywood sheet sliding in the runner grooves. A section through this hatch is shown in Figure 1A. Note how easy it is to make. The runners are bolted to the deck from underneath about ½ inch in from the edge of the hatch opening. The hatch fits into a groove in the runner. The inside face of the deck is finished with a coaming bolted to the header. The header is bolted to the deckhead and the hatch is finished. The slot (S) serves to channel water out of the ends of the hatch and should be carefully caulked.

The washboards on the front of the hatch can be made from waterproof marine-grade plywood. Note how the top panel is made 3 inches to 6 inches (75 mm to 150 mm), and the other panels are equally sized. In rough weather it may be desirable to insert the washboards. By leaving the top one out, a small air gap is left for ventilation. The corner detail

(Figure 1B) shows how to finish the end of the runner. Note how the trim piece is run up past the runner groove to stop the hatch sliding out of the runners. The washboards are dropped into their slot, and when the hatch is closed, the hatch cover slides over the top of the washboards, preventing them from being removed.

A slightly more complex section is shown in Figure 4. This hatch slides on brass plates, which fit into grooves in the side of the runners. Care must be taken to ensure that there is a good seal between the coaming and the side piece, or water will enter.

Figure 3 shows a section through the end of this hatch. Note how the brass slides are stopped by the end of the washboard holder. (This is shown in more detail in Figure 2.) The end piece of the hatch overhangs the washboard slightly, and the plywood hatch cover makes a larger over-

hang to prevent rain from driving into the seal. Also to prevent water entry, the washboards are cut with a slope on their tops and bottoms, as shown here. If additional ventilation is desired, a louvered panel can be built into the plywood washboards (see Chapter 6 for details).

While these hatches are simple to build and reasonably inexpensive, they do have the drawbacks of not being perfectly watertight. Unless great care is taken, they will leak in moderate rains. But I have yet to find a perfectly leakproof hatch on any boat. The type of hatch you install will depend upon the degree of watertightness you require.

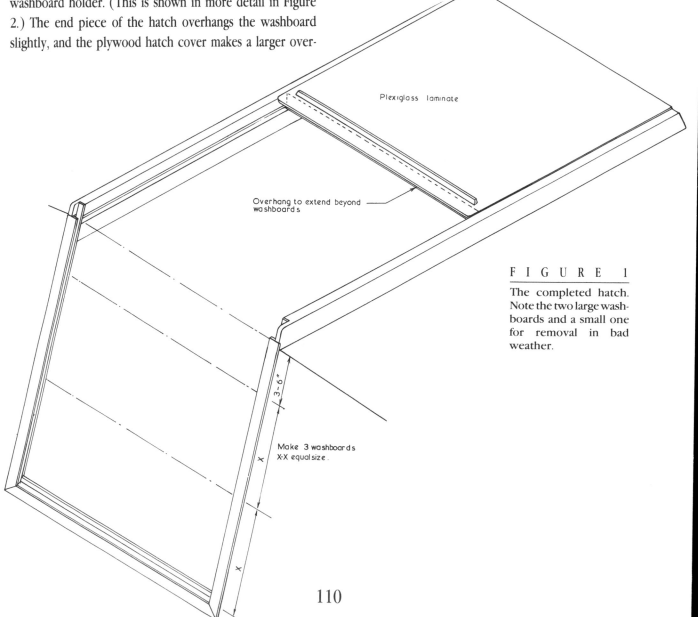

Plexiglass laminate

Overhang to extend beyond washboards

3-6"

Make 3 washboards X-X equal size.

FIGURE 1

The completed hatch. Note the two large washboards and a small one for removal in bad weather.

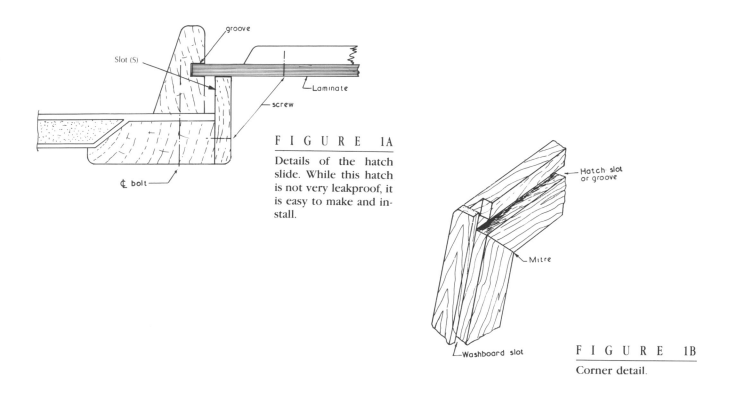

groove

Slot (S)

Laminate

screw

℄ bolt

F I G U R E   1A

Details of the hatch slide. While this hatch is not very leakproof, it is easy to make and install.

Hatch slot or groove

Mitre

Washboard slot

F I G U R E   1B

Corner detail.

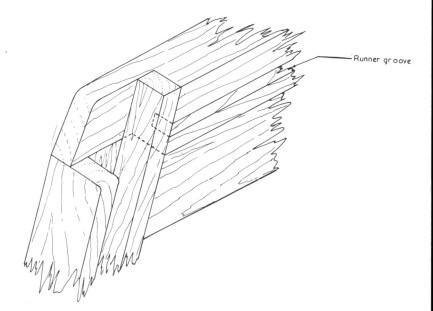

Runner groove

F I G U R E   2

A corner detail showing the method of stopping the hatch from sliding all the way out.

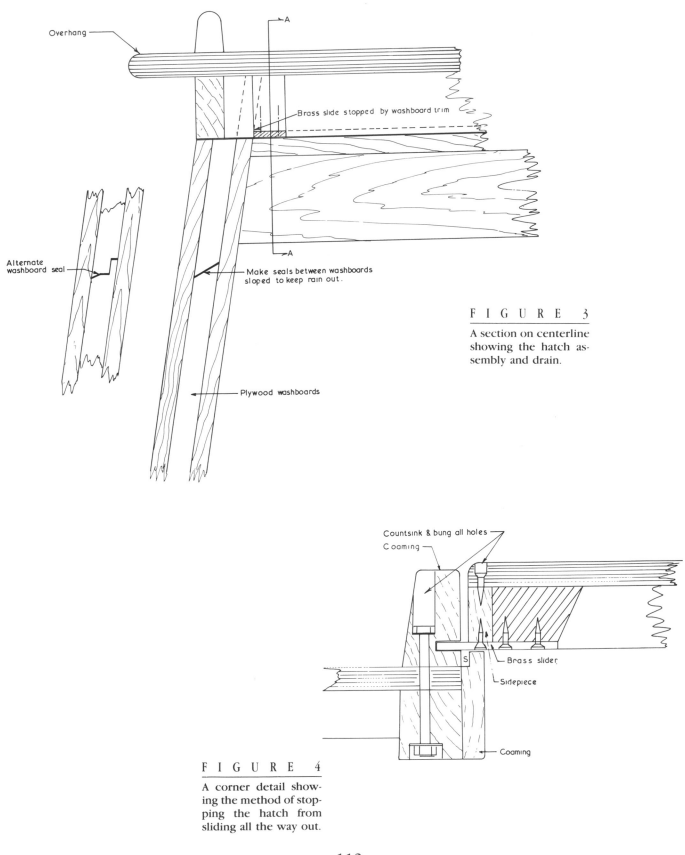

Overhang

Brass slide stopped by washboard trim

Alternate
washboard seal

Make seals between washboards
sloped to keep rain out.

Plywood washboards

F I G U R E 3

A section on centerline
showing the hatch as-
sembly and drain.

Countsink & bung all holes

Coaming

Brass slider

Sidepiece

S

Coaming

F I G U R E 4

A corner detail show-
ing the method of stop-
ping the hatch from
sliding all the way out.

PROJECT 5-2
A REASONABLY WATERTIGHT COMPANIONWAY HATCH

A slightly more watertight version is shown in project 5-2. The hatch shown in Figure 1 has runners specially shaped to fit the curved edge piece. Outside the runners is a second set of longitudinal supports to carry the hatch cover and to stop water from sloshing up and under the runners. Between each set of runners is a groove to channel any water away from the hatch. The washboards of this hatch have a special lap cut to stop any water from getting in. Inset in the washboards are ventilation panels to allow good airflow throughout the boat. Note also that the padlock and hasp are set off to one side of the hatch. If the hasp is set in the center of the hatch, as is often done, it may hit a crewman on the forehead.

For comparison, sections through three hatches are shown in Figures 2, 3, and 4. Figure 2 is a very simple hatch section, which differs from the one shown in Project 5-1 in that a grooved track is bolted to the plywood hatch cover and runs in a groove on the runner. In this case the coaming also serves as a water channel for any water that gets through the hatch. In Figure 3 the runners are made out of pieces of T-track with matching sliders. Ideally the slider runs the entire length of the hatch. Note how the runner is through-bolted through the deck and into the header. On a fiberglass deck the runner and header would be arranged in a similar fashion. However, more caulking would have to be used to ensure a tight seal between the rough side of the fiberglass and the header.

The top section (Figure 4) shows the most complex and watertight arrangement. Half of a brass or plastic pipe runs the entire length of the hatch, as the runner guide. It fits over the plywood hatch sides, protecting the end grain, and is firmly screwed in place. Small brass keys at each corner of the hatch, running in a slot in the runner, serve as additional guides to ensure that the hatch will not twist and jam. Outside the runners are additional runners, which support the hatch cover and serve to keep water out. Note the drain hole in Figure 1 at the end of the cover supports. These are essential to prevent water from being trapped in the end of the hatch cover.

The finished hatch. Note the padlock flange to one side of the hatch and the ventilation openings.

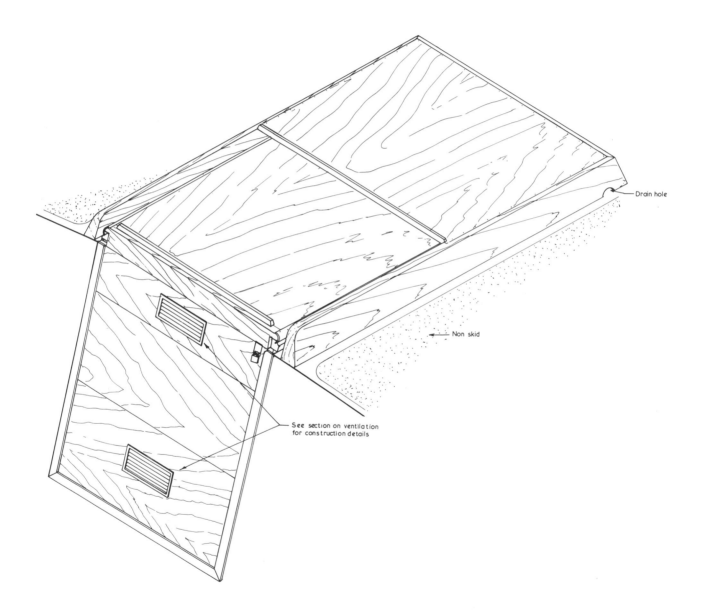

Drain hole

Non skid

See section on ventilation for construction details

F I G U R E   2

A section through a simple hatch.

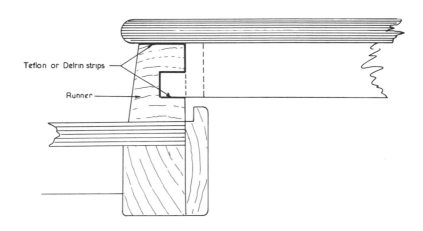

Teflon or Delrin strips

Runner

F I G U R E   3

A section through a more watertight hatch.

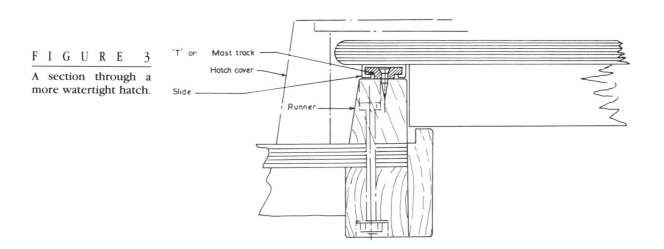

'T' or   Mast track

Hatch cover

Slide

Runner

F I G U R E   4

A section through the most watertight hatch.

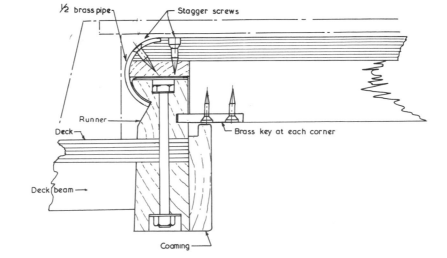

½ brass pipe

Stagger screws

Runner

Deck

Brass key at each corner

Deck beam

Coaming

PROJECT 5 - 3
A FIBERGLASS HATCH COVER

If you have a simple hatch and want to add a hatch cover, there are two ways of building it. One is to make it in wood, as shown in previous drawings. Another is to make it out of fiberglass to match the existing deck. The first step in this process is to measure the hatch carefully and decide on the clearances required. Not enough clearance will jam the hatch; too much will allow rain or seawater to enter. In general, allow about 1 inch (25 mm) above the hatch and, depending on the desired slope of the sides, about 1½ inches (38 mm) on the bottom at the sides. Now carefully draw out the cover on a large piece of cardboard and make a mock-up. This will not only save time in the long run but will ensure that the cover fits correctly without binding.

When the mock-up is satisfactory, it is time to construct a simple mold. This is made from plywood covered with a Formica-like laminate. Figure 1 shows the mold ready to have the cover laid up, and Figure 1A shows a section through the mold. To obtain a smooth finish, the laminate should cover all parts of the mold. Coating the mold with mold-release wax helps to ensure that the cover can be removed from the mold.

To lay up the cover, use three or four alternate layers of 1½-ounce (33 gms/m²) mat and 18-ounce (475 gms/m²) woven roving. Be sure to roll out air bubbles and voids, but do not over-roll. Too much rolling reduces the tensile properties of the material.

When the laminate is dry, the edges can be trimmed and the cover popped out of the mold. Clean up the edges, cut out the drain holes, and the cover is ready to be bolted or screwed into place. Screws should be placed 4 to 6 inches (100 mm to 150 mm) apart. If you wish to coat the top of the cover with nonskid or paint it to match the deck, this work should be done before bolting the cover down. Figure 2 shows the cover screwed into place.

Other methods of improving hatches are to add a screen as shown in Figure 3, and to add dodger grooves. Methods of making your own screens are explained in Chapter 6.

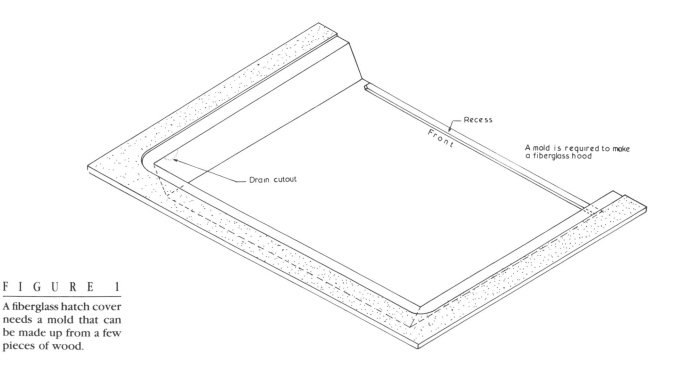

A mold is required to make a fiberglass hood

Recess

Front

Drain cutout

F I G U R E 1

A fiberglass hatch cover needs a mold that can be made up from a few pieces of wood.

FIGURE 1A

A section through the mold for the fiberglass hatch cover.

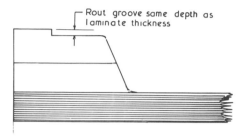

Rout groove same depth as laminate thickness

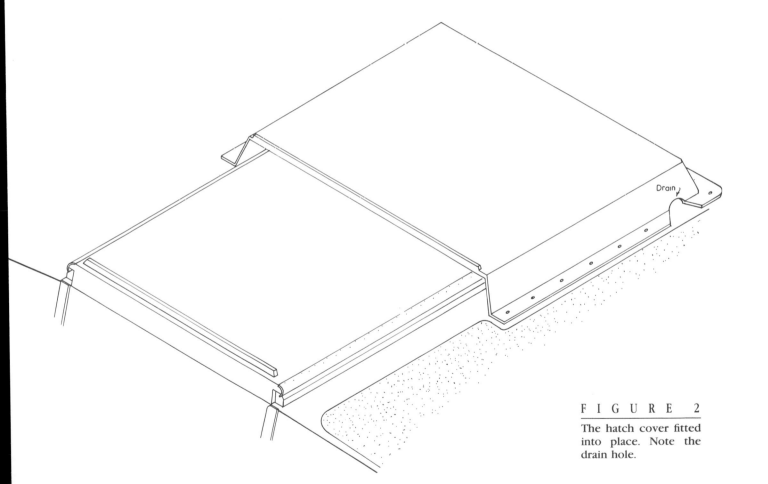

FIGURE 2

The hatch cover fitted into place. Note the drain hole.

Drain

F I G U R E 3

A simply made screen can be inserted in place of the washboards.

FOREDECK HATCHES

Suppose you want to build a foredeck hatch or enlarge your present hatch because the sails won't fit through it. The first question you should ask yourself is, How large a hatch do I need? Figure 5-1 shows a chart I developed for an earlier book called *Designed to Win*. This chart is based on the mast height or *I* dimension, the distance from the mast to the headstay along the deck, or the *J* dimension, and the total sail area. Using it, you should be able to find the size of hatch that will allow the sails for your boat to pass through easily.

Having found the best size, the next job is to decide on the type of hatch you would like to install. Should it be a sliding hatch? A lifting hatch? Should the hatch cover be completely removable, or should it open from either side? Will the hatch be used for sails only, sails and people, or people only?

Most hatches are used for both sails and people, and very few have hatch covers that are completely removable. So that leaves us with the option of a sliding or lifting hatch. I prefer sliding hatches, so we'll look at these first.

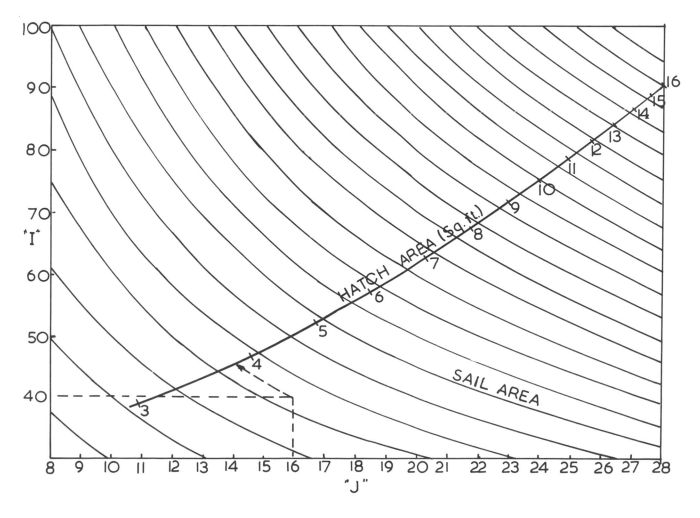

PROJECT 5-4
A SLIDING FOREDECK HATCH

I once raced on a boat with a spinnaker pole fixed to the mast. The boat also had a centerline hatch with a lifting lid. Unfortunately, the two do not go together. The only time we could open the hatch was when the spinnaker was set or when the inboard end of the pole was raised as high as it would go. On a racing boat such a loss of efficiency could cost several trophies. On a shorthanded cruising boat the price could be higher. It could cost the headsail if the hatch cannot be opened to stuff the sail down in bad weather, or it could even cost you a crewman. For this reason, a sliding hatch makes good sense.

Figure 1 shows the simplest of sliding hatches. It is reasonably watertight, easy to make, and relatively inexpensive. It consists of two runners and a hatch that slides in the runners. The hatch is held in the runners by means of brass keys set in the corners of the hatch. Figure 1B shows a section through the side of this hatch (at *BB*). Note the groove in the coaming to channel water away. The forward and aft ends of the hatch also require special attention. Figure 1A shows a section through the front face of the hatch (at *AA*). Note the drain hole, foam rubber gasket, and slot for the padlock. If you do not want to padlock this hatch, it can be fastened from inside. The crosspiece is bolted firmly to the deck, and the hatch butts tightly up against it. The rubber gasket and the drain hole keep most of the water from going below. However, this is not a totally watertight hatch, no matter how well it is built.

Figure 1C shows a section (at *CC*) of the hatch at the aft end of the opening. Note the foam rubber gasket. In this drawing a hatch cover is shown. I prefer to have covers on foredeck hatches simply to make them more watertight, as they are located in a wet area of the boat. Finally Figure 1D shows a section through the back wall of the hatch (at *DD*), illustrating the hatch cover and foam rubber stop. Figure 2 shows the hatch with the cover added, and Figure 2A shows a section through the side of this hatch with the cover in place. Note how the hatch opening is faced with a coaming, which, if you want the hatch to look nice, could be a piece of mahogany or teak. Note also the rounded inner corners on the coaming.

Above deck outside the coaming is the runner. It has a groove cut in the inside face to enable the hatch to slide easily. The groove is about ¼-inch (6 mm) wide and ½-inch (12 mm) deep. The runner is held to the deck and blocking by either gluing and bolting or caulking and bolting. For an average-size hatch the bolts should be about ⅜ inch (9 mm) in diameter, but if other sizes look better, make your own decision about size.

The hatch is made out of mahogany or teak and is a simple box about 2 or 3 inches (50 mm or 75 mm) high. The top can be solid Lexcan or Plexiglas, or it can be plywood, depending on how much light you want below. Note that each part should be either firmly glued or caulked to its neighbor to make it as watertight as possible.

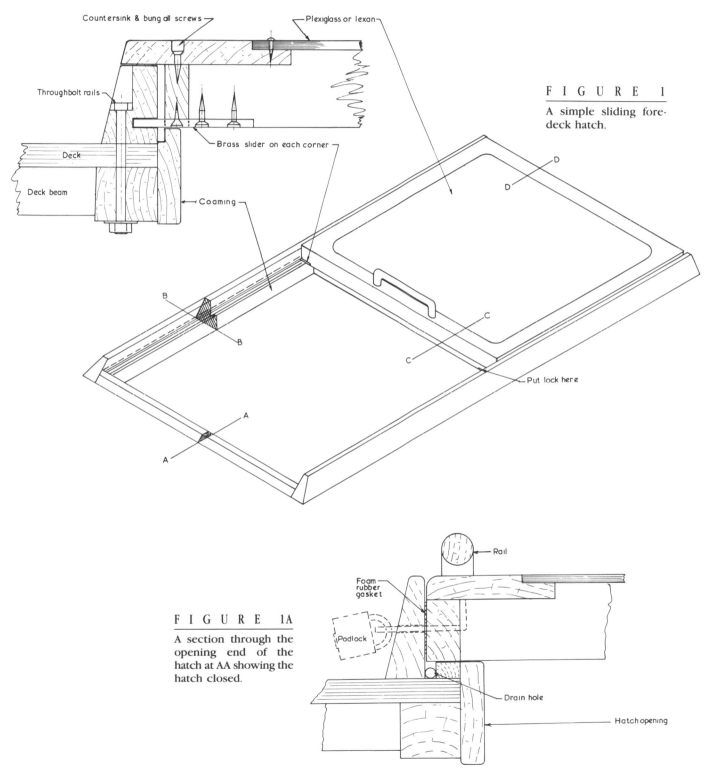

F I G U R E   1B

A section through the hatch at BB showing the slider and rails.

Countersink & bung all screws

Plexiglass or lexan

Throughbolt rails

Brass slider on each corner

Deck

Deck beam

Coaming

F I G U R E   1

A simple sliding foredeck hatch.

D

D

B

B

C

C

A

A

Put lock here

F I G U R E   1A

A section through the opening end of the hatch at AA showing the hatch closed.

Rail

Foam rubber gasket

Padlock

Drain hole

Hatch opening

F I G U R E   1C

A section through the hatch at CC showing it closed.

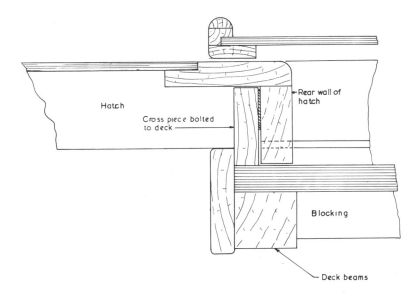

Hatch

Cross piece bolted to deck

Rear wall of hatch

Blocking

Deck beams

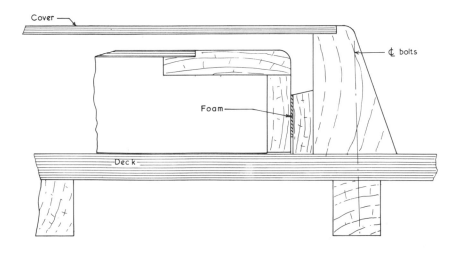

Cover

¢ bolts

Foam

Deck

F I G U R E   1D

Section DD at the end of the hatch, showing it open.

122

The hatch open showing a simple plywood cover.

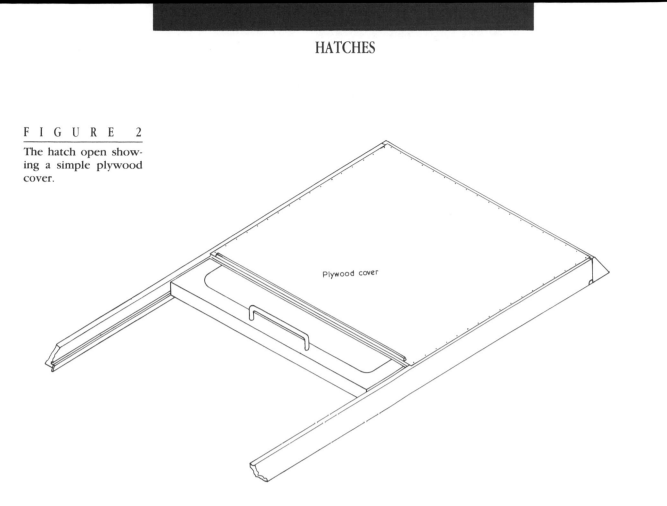

Plywood cover

F I G U R E   2A

Detail showing how the plywood cover is fitted.

Plywood cover

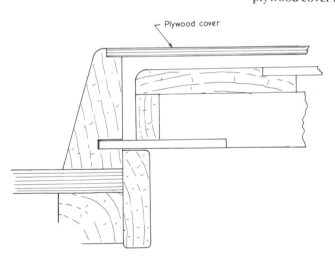

PROJECT 5 - 5
A HINGED FOREDECK HATCH

If you prefer a hinged foredeck hatch, here's a beauty. The hatch opening is surrounded by a low sill with its own gutter. The lid seals the entire unit when it is closed and can be dogged down against the rubber gasket around the sill. By using hinges with removable pins at each end, the hatch can be made to open in either direction or, with dogs or barrel bolts, it can be securely locked from inside.

Figure 1 shows the hatch fitted into a wooden deck, but the principle is similar if it is to be fitted on a fiberglass deck. First the hatch must be sized and measured. Make drawings and cardboard mock-ups before cutting any wood. Next cut the hole in the deck. It should be the width of the coaming larger than the size of the finished opening. In other words, if you are going to use a coaming ¾-inch (18 mm) thick, the hole should be cut 1½ inches (36 mm) larger than the desired finished size. On a wooden boat the deck beams will have to be jointed to a header running fore and aft. On a fiberglass deck the entire opening should be framed in with wood blocking. The blocking should be bedded in caulking and screwed through the deck. Figure 1A shows a section through a wooden deck. A section through a fiberglass deck is shown in Figure 2. Next glue and screw the coaming to the blocking. Add a small spacer (E) and an external trim (D), which both covers the screw holes and makes a gutter to channel water away. Note that the gutter must have drain holes in the corners.

With the hatch opening sized and fitted it is time to make the hatch cover. Sections through the hatch cover are also shown in Figures 1 and 2. Figure 3 shows an exploded view of the hatch cover. Part B must be square and glued and screwed firmly together. The hatch sides are glued and screwed to the frame, and a small reinforcing block (C) is added. When the hatch frame is finished, it should be varnished or painted and then the Plexiglas or smoked Lexcan screwed in place. You can use plywood instead of plastic, but the plastic will give more light in the forepeak. A handle, preferably wood, should be bolted to the frame of the hatch (Part B) for easy opening.

Assembly of both parts is relatively easy. First, ensure that the hinges are spaced correctly and at the correct height and that the hatch will open when they are bolted down. You may have to shave a little off the coaming to enable the hatch to lift easily. The hatch should lie almost flat on the deck when open. (The handle will prevent it from lying perfectly flat.) Finally, add the remaining hardware, such as barrel bolts or dogs, to keep the hatch locked, and lay nonskid where desired over the transparent plastic. Figure 3 shows the positioning of the nonskid. Figure 4 shows the hatch fully installed and open.

HATCHES

FIGURE 1

The installation of the hatch in a wooden deck. Note blocking and method of ending deck beams.

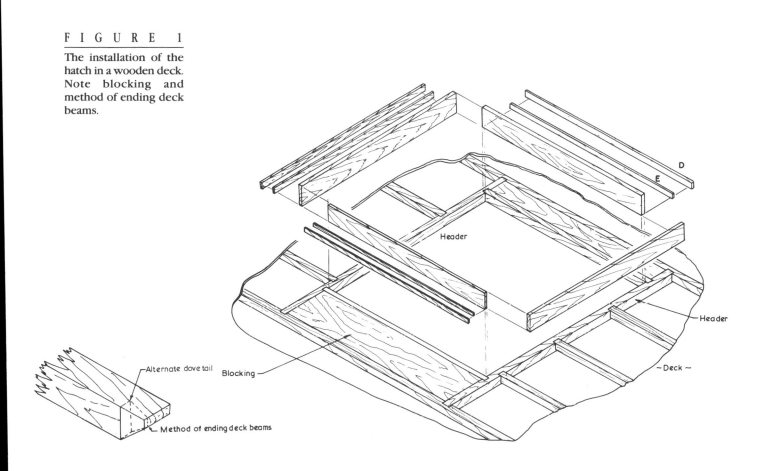

Alternate dove tail

Method of ending deck beams

Blocking

Header

Header

Deck

D

E

FIGURE 1A

A section through the hatch cover showing foam gasket and screwing details.

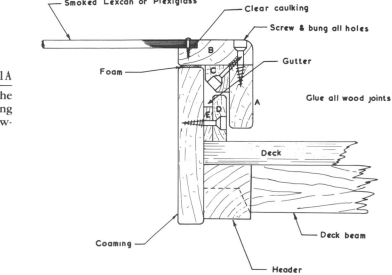

Smoked Lexcan or Plexiglass

Clear caulking

Screw & bung all holes

Foam

Gutter

Glue all wood joints

B

C

A

E

D

Deck

Coaming

Deck beam

Header

F I G U R E 2

A section showing how a hatch is installed in a foam-cored deck. The foam is stripped out in way of the hatch and tapered. The two fiberglass laminates are then joined and blocked with wood. Then the hatch is built.

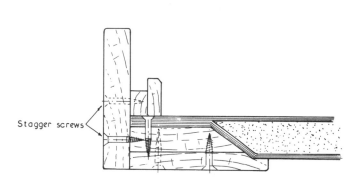

Stagger screws

Alternate corner joint

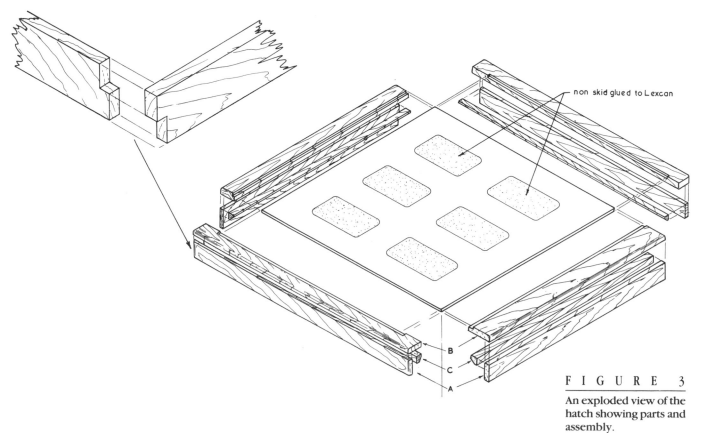

non skid glued to Lexcan

B
C
A

F I G U R E 3

An exploded view of the hatch showing parts and assembly.

126

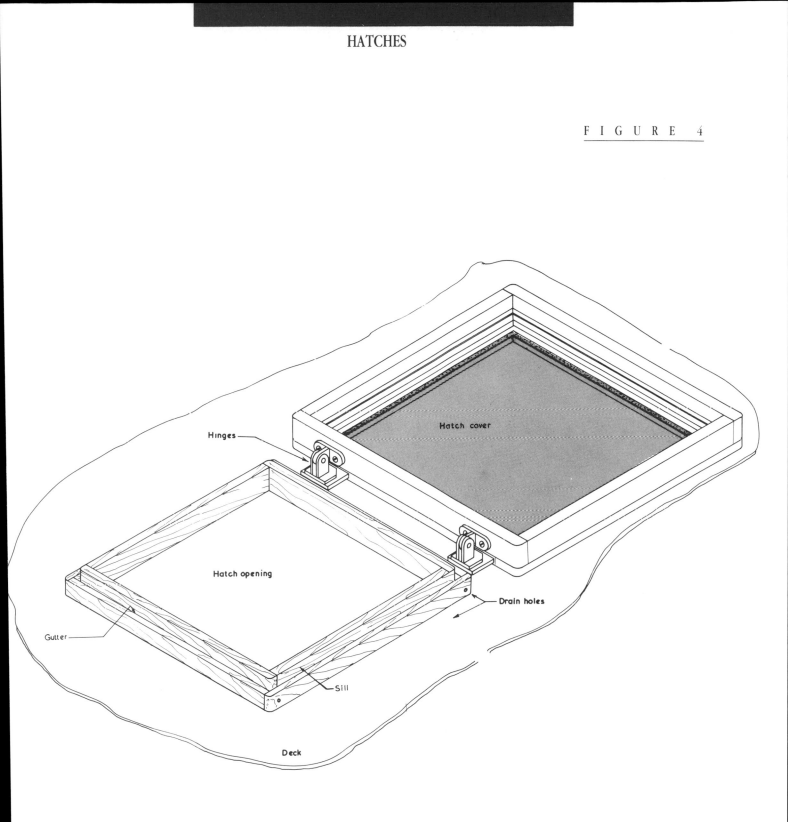

Hatch cover

Hinges

Hatch opening

Drain holes

Gutter

Sill

Deck

PROJECT 5 - 6
MAKING AND INSTALLING
A SKYLIGHT

How often have you looked at an older traditional yacht and admired the skylights and brightly varnished finish work? Here's a drawing showing the essentials of constructing a traditional skylight.

Look first at the exploded view in Figure 7. It shows the various parts of the skylight before they are assembled. There are many possible variations in the joints that can be used. Individual builders can modify the plan to suit their level of skill and experience.

Figure 1 of Project 5-6 shows the skylight fully assembled. Sections through it are shown in Figures 2, 3, 4, and 5. Figure 6 shows how the hatch is mounted on a fiberglass deck. Note that the deck core is cut away, and the upper and lower laminates are glassed together.

To make this skylight, draw all the pieces at full scale and cut to suit. (Scale drawings are not shown because the size of the skylight can vary greatly.) Assemble the skylight by building the box structure first. This uses parts A and B in Figure 1 and Figure 7. Note the corner joints. These can be dovetailed, lapped, or simply butted. The dovetailed joints are probably the strongest, but also the most difficult to make. Figures 1A and 1B show two of the possible options. When the box is first made, it should be fitted into the hole or placed on the deck around the hole to make sure it is sized correctly. Note that the sections shown in Figures 2 and 3 show the hatch passing through the deck. In many cases this is easier than sitting the hatch on the deck and covering the deck edge with trim, as shown in Figure 2A. But often, if the joint is not perfect, water will penetrate. If you anticipate that your joints will be less than perfect, the method shown in 2A may be better. In any case, the edges should be caulked carefully and a trim piece or quarter round added all around the skylight, as shown in Figure 4. At this stage you should paint or varnish the base unit.

When you are happy with the fit of the skylight, make the opening panels. Make the frame by gluing and screwing the sides and ends together. Check the diagonals for squareness and make sure there is no twist in the unit. Once again, you should varnish or paint each panel at this stage. Then install the translucent plastic (or glass) and hold it in place by nailing a quarter round strip all around its edge. If you wish to make the plastic flush with the top of the hatch, it will have to be screwed to the wooden frame. While this method prevents water accumulation at the bottom of the plastic, it is more difficult to keep watertight.

Now add the brass rods. You might want to lacquer them to stop discoloration, but eventually lacquer will peel and they will discolor. The brass rods serve to prevent large objects smashing the glass and may be omitted if you use Plexiglas or Lexcan. I feel, however, that they epitomize the character of such a hatch and should be included. Note that the bars are held captive by the end pieces (C), as shown in Figure 3. Therefore, the holes for the brass rods should be drilled only halfway into the end pieces.

The panels will hinge on the central bar. Figure 3 shows a section through this bar. Note the gutter to channel any leaks out the side of the skylight. While this center piece is shown as one unit, it might be easier to make it from several pieces.

Finally, add the rods and clamps used to hold the panels open, as shown in Figure 5, as well as any trim pieces. Make sure the skylight opens smoothly and that the opening panels can be fixed in any position. The job is now completed. On older boats, skylights were often positioned under the dinghy. If you decide to do this, the chocks shown in Chapter 7 would support the dinghy clear of the skylight.

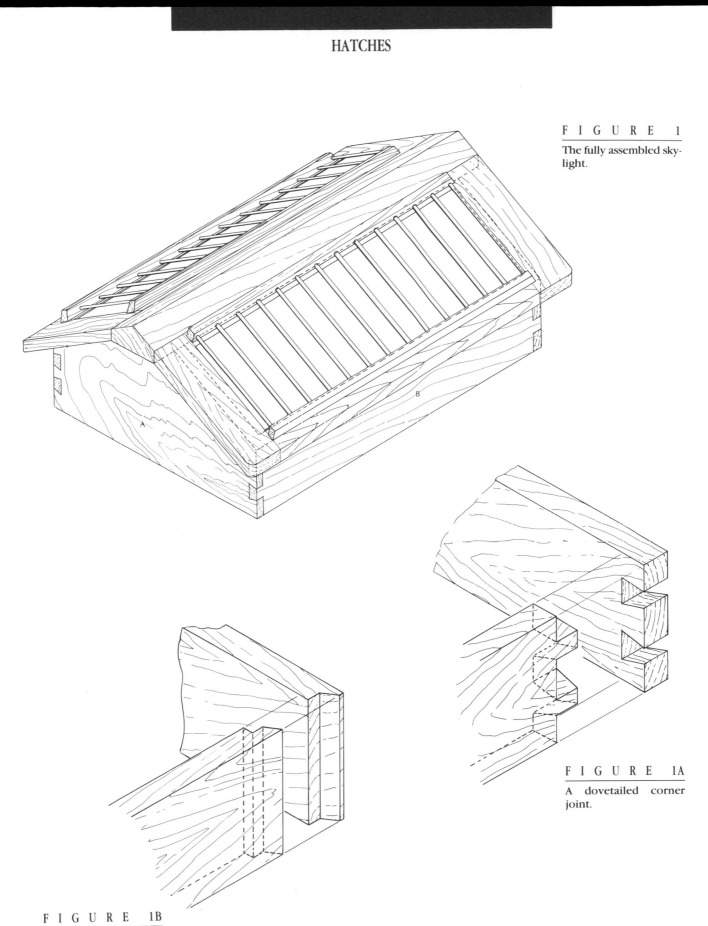

F I G U R E   1A

A dovetailed corner
joint.

F I G U R E   1B

An alternate corner
joint.

129

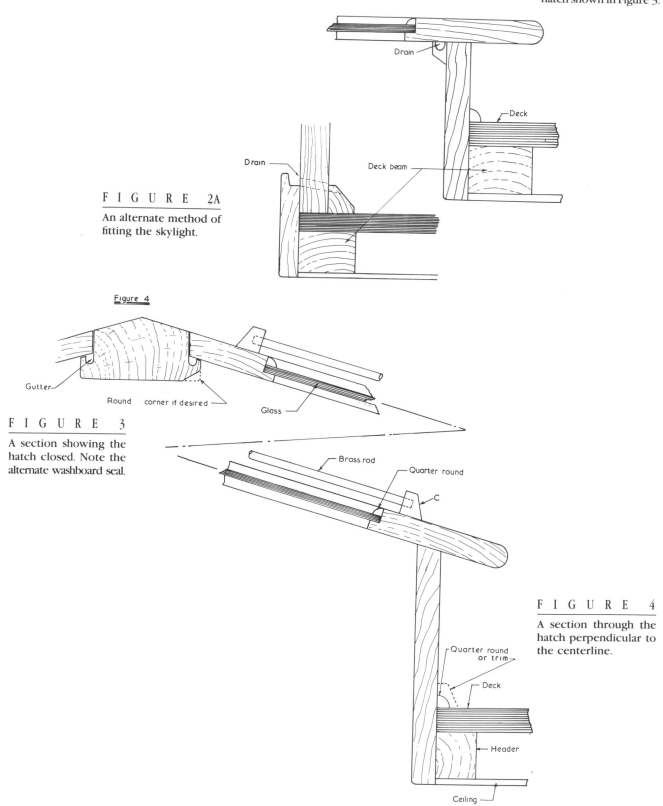

FIGURE 2

Section AA through the hatch shown in Figure 3.

Drain

Deck

Drain

Deck beam

FIGURE 2A

An alternate method of fitting the skylight.

Figure 4

Gutter

Round   corner if desired

Glass

FIGURE 3

A section showing the hatch closed. Note the alternate washboard seal.

Brass rod

Quarter round

C

FIGURE 4

A section through the hatch perpendicular to the centerline.

Quarter round
or trim

Deck

Header

Ceiling

FIGURE 5
Detail of the opening rod. These can be made or purchased from a good furniture-hardware store.

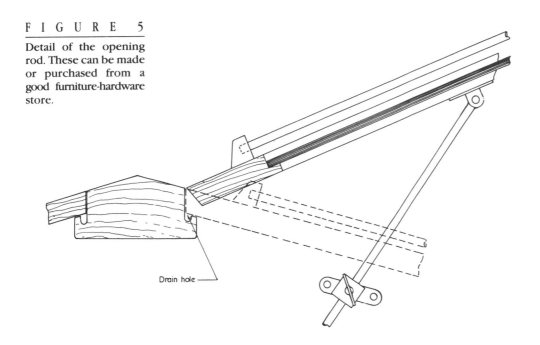

Drain hole

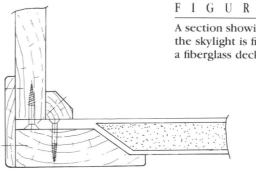

FIGURE 6

A section showing how the skylight is fitted on a fiberglass deck.

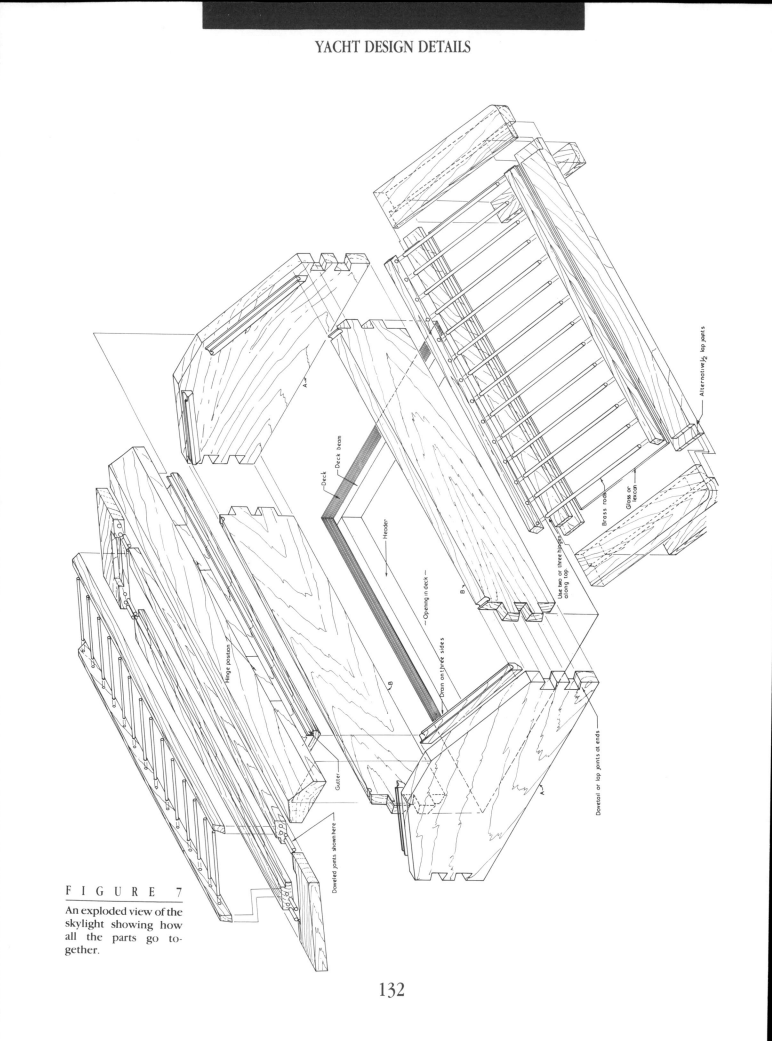

Alternative 1/2 lap joints

Glass or lexan

Brass rods

Use two or three hinges along top

Deck beam

Deck

Header

Opening in deck

Drain on three sides

Dowetail or lap joints at ends

Hinge position

Gutter

Doweled joints shown here

F I G U R E   7

An exploded view of the skylight showing how all the parts go together.

A TRADITIONAL MAIN COMPANIONWAY HATCH

For many sailors the modern companionway leaves much to be desired. The washboards get misplaced or the hatch is not high enough. Often it is badly made or not very watertight. If you have these complaints about your boat, consider installing a traditional main companionway hatch. Figure 1 shows the finished hatchway.

By tapering the runners or hatch logs, the hatch can be raised several inches without appearing to be. The curved hatch cover increases height even more. It has a very traditional look, and if it is caulked, it will look even more authentic. The paneled wooden doors are made to be left in place or removed as desired. If you want the ultimate in comfort, a screen door can be fitted behind the wooden doors.

To make this unit, size and cut the hatch logs or runners. Then bolt them to the hatch sides. Figure 2 shows a section through the detail at the end of the hatch while Figure 3 shows the hatch sides. Note the drip groove and coaming, which serves to cover the end of the deck. Next make the two ends of the hatch—pieces A and B in Figure 4. If they are cut together, they will be matched. The next step is to glue and screw the ¼-inch plywood to the curved side of pieces A and B. Add the side pieces (D), and glue and backscrew the longitudinal strips (E) to the plywood. At this point, the hatch should sit comfortably on the runners. Check to make sure everything fits well, and then remove the hatch and add the brass track (F). The holes should be drilled, but the screws left out at the lower end so that the hatch can be lifted over the stop at the aft end. Now the hatch can be slid onto the runners. Lift the lower end over the stop and screw the brass strips in place. Add stops (wooden blocks) at the lower end to prevent the track from hitting the deck. The upper end will be stopped by the trim strips surrounding the doors.

The doors are made in the same style as traditional paneled doors for houses. The various framework pieces are assembled by fitting their slots over the tapered edged panels, as shown in Figure 5. Add the handles, hinges, and any other brasswork that you may want, and install the doors. The stop at the top of each door should be carefully positioned so that the door closes without jamming at the top. If you wish to add a screen door, the procedure is explained in Chapter 6.

These are just a few of the methods of making hatches, skylights, and companionways. Hopefully, they will stimulate ideas from which your own designs will develop. Keep in mind that adding a well-made hatch or a skylight to your boat could not only make it more attractive and comfortable but could increase its resale value.

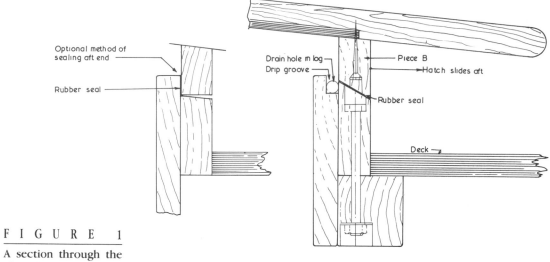

Optional method of sealing aft end

Rubber seal

Drain hole in log
Drip groove
Piece B
Hatch slides aft
Rubber seal
Deck

F I G U R E 1

A section through the aft end of the hatch.

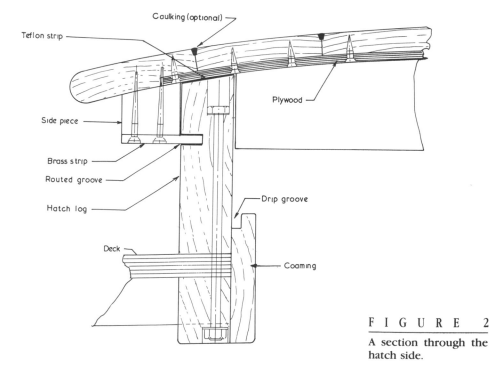

Caulking (optional)
Teflon strip
Plywood
Side piece
Brass strip
Routed groove
Hatch log
Drip groove
Deck
Coaming

F I G U R E 2

A section through the hatch side.

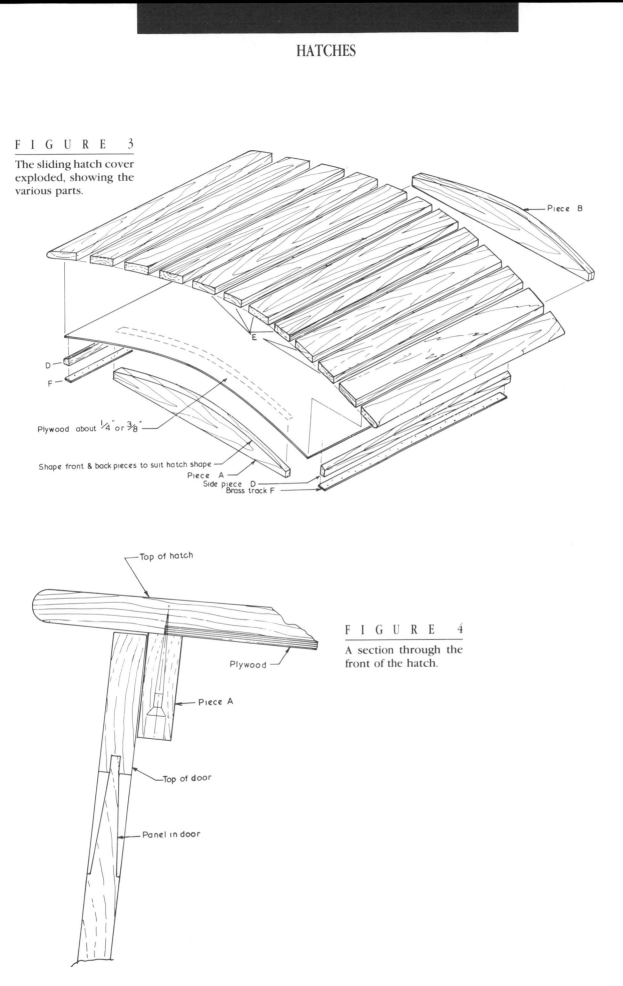

FIGURE 3

The sliding hatch cover exploded, showing the various parts.

Piece B

E

D

F

Plywood about 1/4" or 3/8"

Shape front & back pieces to suit hatch shape

Piece A

Side piece D

Brass track F

Top of hatch

FIGURE 4

A section through the front of the hatch.

Plywood

Piece A

Top of door

Panel in door

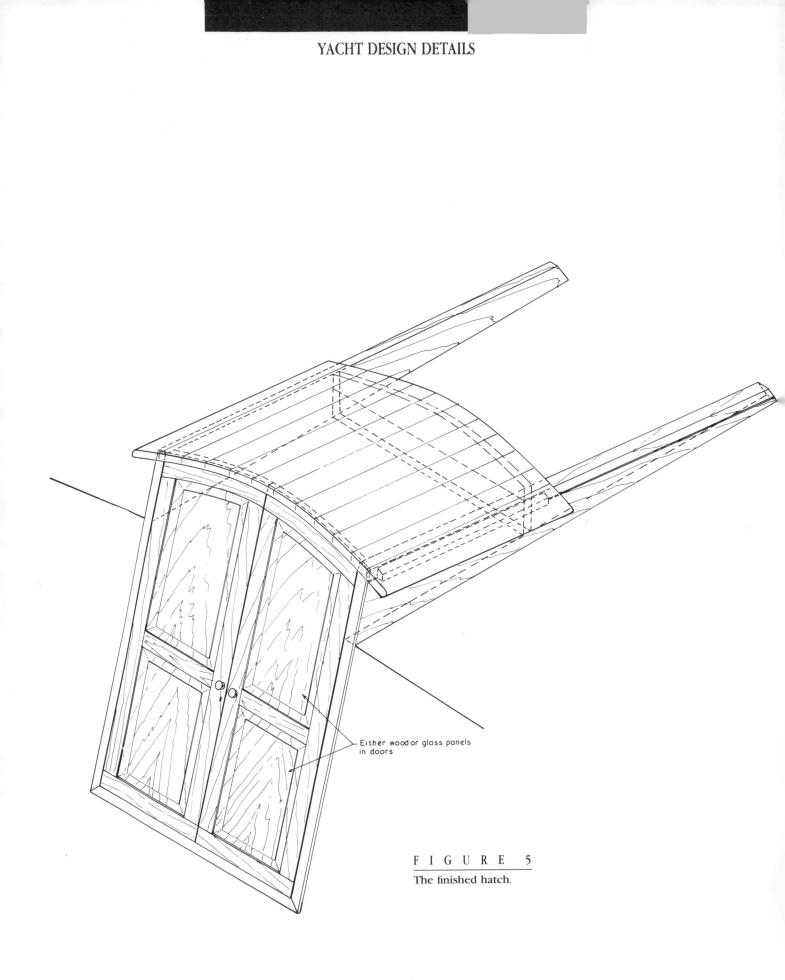

Either wood or glass panels in doors

F I G U R E   5

The finished hatch.

CHAPTER 6

VENTILATION

Without adequate ventilation the interior of a boat will become mildewed and musty. Fortunately there are many ways of improving ventilation belowdecks. The simplest is to leave all locker doors open. More complicated methods range from installing a solar-powered Nicro Fico vent, as shown in Project 6-5, Figure 7, to forced-air ventilation throughout the boat.

Should you choose to leave locker doors open, they will have to be fastened with a catch or wedge to ensure that they stay open. A better idea is to install louvers, either in a panel or as a complete door.

PROJECT 6-1
LOUVERED DOORS

Louvered doors are quite easy to make. They require a small amount of skill and plenty of patience. Most of the parts can be bought already planed to size, and all you have to do is cut the pieces to the right length and assemble them. One method of obtaining the slats for the doors is to purchase a set of wooden venetian blinds. These are made in various standard sizes and are often on sale. The slats can easily be removed from the blind and cut to the desired length.

MAKING THE LOUVERED PANEL

It is best to think of this job in two steps. The first step is to make the louvered panel and the second is to fit the panel into the door. If the entire door is to be louvered, then the second stage is redundant.

Project 6-1 shows each step separately. You must first

137

make the vertical side pieces to hold the louvers at the right angle. These can be made in several ways. Measure the thickness of the door in which the panel is to be installed. The end piece (A in the exploded view, Figure 6) should be no thicker than the door, unless you intend to trim it carefully to hide the increased thickness. Figure 1 shows how this width affects the width of the louvers and their spacing. If there is a ½-inch (12 mm) space between louvers set at a 30-degree angle, there will be a small gap, depending upon the size of the louvers, as shown in A. This allows the contents of the locker to be seen. It would be better to use a ⅜-inch (9.5 mm) space. B shows this space with the louvers set at a 45-degree angle.

SPACING THE LOUVERS

In Figure 2, wooden strips are used to space the louvers correctly. The wood is clamped at the correct angle, either 30 or 45 degrees, and sawn off flush with the edge of the frame. A ⅜-inch by ⅜-inch (9.5 mm × 9.5 mm) batten is suitable for the size shown in Figure 1. If a smaller or larger gap is required, use a different size piece of wood. Each strip is glued and tacked in place.

This leaves the end of the wooden spacers showing. Therefore, a trim piece (B in the exploded view in Figure 6) must be installed to cover the ends and hold the louvers in place. To finish the ends, use small triangular pieces (C in the exploded view).

If you own a table saw or router, use it to cut out the grooves instead of using spacer strips between the louvers. Figure 3 shows how the grooves would appear after being cut with a table saw. The cuts are clean and ready for the louvers to be installed. Note that this method also requires a trim strip to cover the end of the grooves and to hold the louvers in place.

Figure 4 shows how the grooves can be cut using a plunge router. Each groove is just large enough to hold the louver strip firmly in place. This method usually will not require a trim strip, unless you make a mistake.

To assemble the panel, first make a dry run to ensure that everything fits. (Note: If the panel is to be painted, all the components should be primed and undercoated at this stage. Then, when assembly is completed, the entire unit can be sprayed with topcoat.) The side piece should be laid flat on the bench and the louvers fitted. Next fit the other side piece. The panel will be reasonably flexible at this point. Now you can position clamps and get the glue ready. If the louvers are smaller than the length of the groove, you may have to shim the underside slightly with a piece of cardboard, otherwise the louvers will be flush on one side and set back on the other. Now each louver can be glued in place and the whole unit clamped. Remember to check for squareness and twist before the glue sets.

FINISHING THE PANEL

Now fit the top and bottom pieces (T in Figure 6). Again check for squareness. These pieces should be glued and nailed or screwed in place. Depending on the type of door panel you are making, it may be time to add the trim pieces. If the panel is to be set into an existing door, then the trim pieces (B) are added later. But if you are making an entire door, the trim pieces should be fitted as soon as all the louvers are secured and the glue is dry.

FITTING THE PANEL IN A DOOR

Before removing the door from the boat, make sure that the louver panel will get adequate air moving past it and that it will not interfere with other fittings close by. With the door laid flat on the workbench, measure the position of the panel carefully. (An experienced builder will work out everything by measurement and then lay the panel over the measurement marks to ensure that no mistakes have been made.) Drill a small hole in the area to be cut out and, using a keyhole or jig saw, carefully cut out the opening. When the opening has been cut, dry-fit the panel until a satisfactory fit is obtained. Only then should the panel be glued in place.

When the panel is firmly glued in place, the trim pieces can be fitted. Make sure they cover the entire cutout and the ends of the wood strips, as shown in Figure 5. They should be glued and nailed in place using finish nails. With this work done, all that remains is to varnish or paint the door. Figure 6 shows an exploded view of the door with all the pieces ready to be fitted.

WHERE TO FIT THE PANELS

Figure 7 shows various positions where louvered panels can be fitted into existing doors. The topmost door has a fully louvered panel. The only drawback to this is the possibility that someone may fall against it and go right through. With a topvent only, air has to enter the locker at the bottom of the door for adequate ventilation. So in this case, you should leave a slight gap at the bottom of the door. The best design is the door shown at the bottom, where air can easily flow in at the bottom and out at the top.

F I G U R E   1

The dimensions of a louvered panel must be carefully laid out to ensure that no gaps are present. In A the slats are laid on a 60-degree slope ½ inch (12 mm) apart, and a small gap is present. In B the slats are laid ⅜ inch (9 mm) apart at a 45-degree angle with no gap.

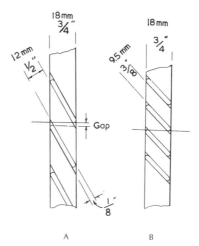

A   B

F I G U R E   2

If strips of wood are used to space the slats, they can be nailed to the frame and sawn off.

F I G U R E   3

An alternative method is to cut grooves for the slats using a table saw or router.

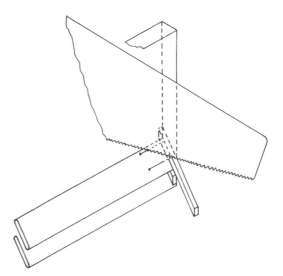

139

F I G U R E 4

A third method is to use a plunge router and keep the slats totally captive.

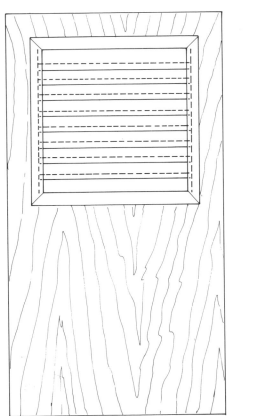

F I G U R E 5

A typical door and section showing a vent panel high in the door.

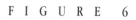

An exploded view of the panel assembly.

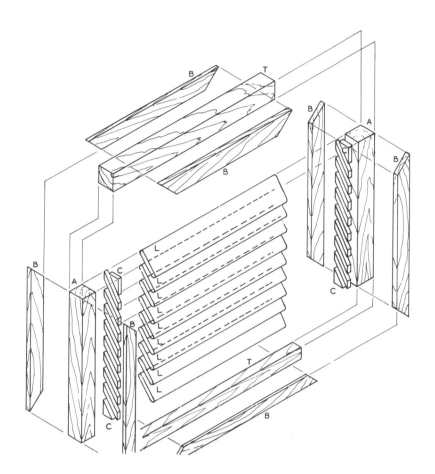

F I G U R E 7

Different positions for the vents.

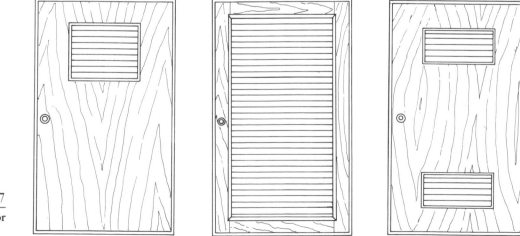

MAKING A DOOR WITH
ADJUSTABLE LOUVERS

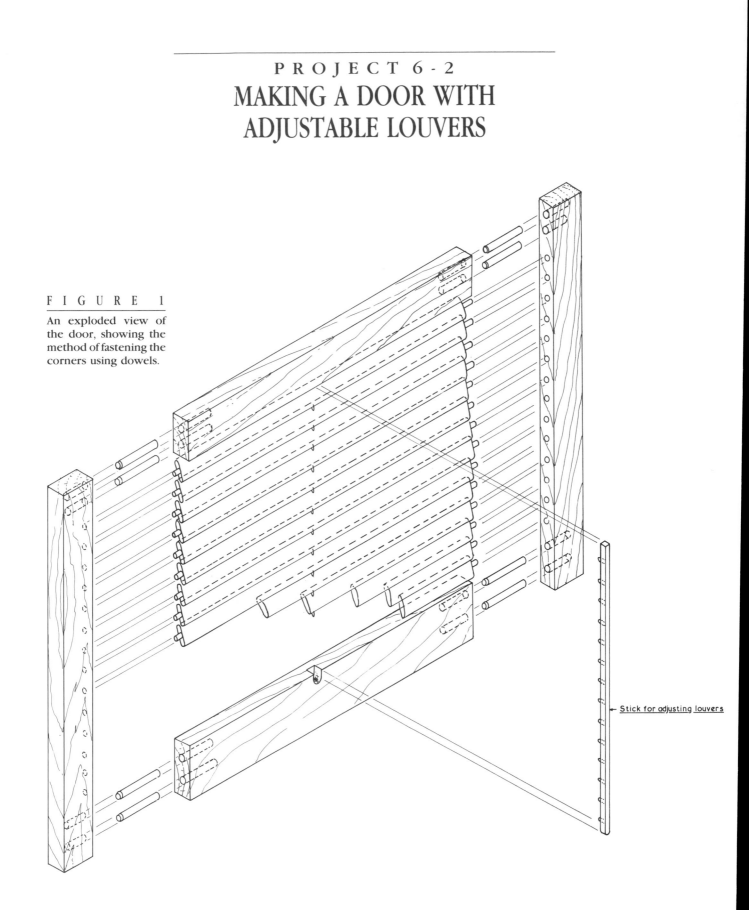

F I G U R E   1
An exploded view of the door, showing the method of fastening the corners using dowels.

Stick for adjusting louvers

The previous project showed how to make a door with fixed louvers. This project shows the construction of a door (or window) with adjustable louvers. Either the louver slats must be purchased with dowels at each end or the dowels shoould be turned on a lathe. The louvers may be adjusted by either a string or a wooden rod mounted in the middle of the panel. The rod is attached to the louvers by means of small staples inserted into both the rod and the louver. If you use string, it can be knotted on either side of a small hole drilled in the louver. Both these jobs are easier to read about than to actually do, but once you have made the louvers, the rest is quite simple.

ASSEMBLY

If the side pieces have not been drilled to fit the louver ends, they must be carefully marked and drilled at the desired depth and distance. Make sure you use a drill bit large enough to allow the louvers to expand in the humidity of the boat. Figure 1, the exploded view, shows the assembly of the panel. First, mount the top and bottom pieces on one of the sides. Glue and screw these pieces in place. Install each louver slat on the same side piece. Now position the other side piece and align the louvers with their correct holes. The whole

F I G U R E 2

The assembled door. Note the stick for adjusting the slats.

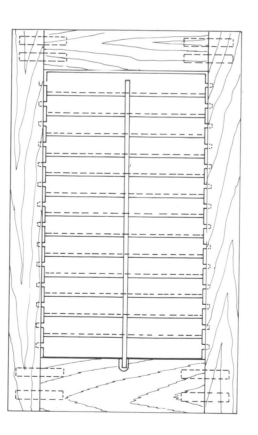

unit should be glued and clamped. Again check the panel is square and perfectly flat before leaving the glue to set. Figure 2 shows a front view and a section through the panel with all the pieces in their place.

With the panel assembled, follow the procedure for installing it in a door as explained in the previous section. Be sure that the doors are not located where the louvers are likely to be damaged when they are opened or closed.

The adjustment rod is attached individually to each slat by staples. Nail staples to the rod the same distance apart as the louvers. Now pass another staple through each staple and nail it to the louver, as shown in the drawing. Make sure you nail the staples in tightly or they may fall out when the vent is used. Figure 3 shows an alternative method of adjusting the slats. It uses a light line attached to small sheaves or rollers at the top and bottom of the door. While this is slightly more complex to install, it makes for a neater finish.

FIGURE 3

An alternative method of adjusting the slats. The string or rope runs around the pulley at the top of the door and hangs down beside the door. A light line connects each slat. When the string is pulled, the pulley turns and moves the light line, which opens the door.

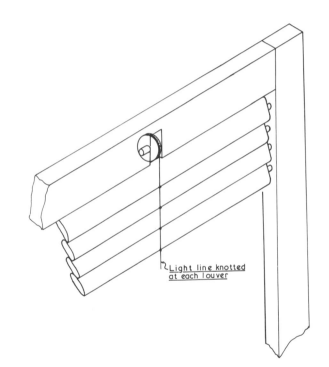

Light line knotted at each louver

P R O J E C T 6 - 3
MAKING A SCREENED DOOR

Among the methods of increasing the ventilation inside a boat, screens over hatches and doors are easy to make and keep out undesirable insects. Screens are often made to be fitted from the inside of the boat, but that can often pose problems. For instance, a screen made to fit under a foredeck hatch will require some method of fastening it to the underside of the hatch. It must also be easily removable to allow the hatch to be closed and should have a tight seal around the edge. Figure 1 shows a typical screen looking up from below. Figure 1A shows a section through a simple toggle clamp used to hold the hatch in place. In the section shown in Figure 1B the hatch is simply rested on top of the opening and gravity holds it in place. While this is quite adequate if the boat is in a marina, it is not recommended for use at sca.

Smaller screens can be made to suit ports if they are not already supplied by the manufacturer. Figure 2 shows an easily constructed port screen. In this case the unit consists

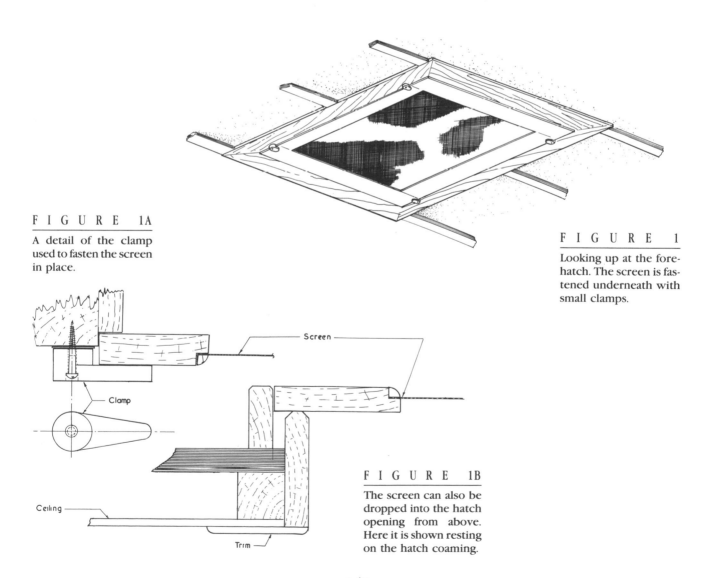

F I G U R E 1A

A detail of the clamp used to fasten the screen in place.

F I G U R E 1

Looking up at the fore-hatch. The screen is fastened underneath with small clamps.

Screen

Clamp

Ceiling

Trim

F I G U R E 1B

The screen can also be dropped into the hatch opening from above. Here it is shown resting on the hatch coaming.

F I G U R E   2

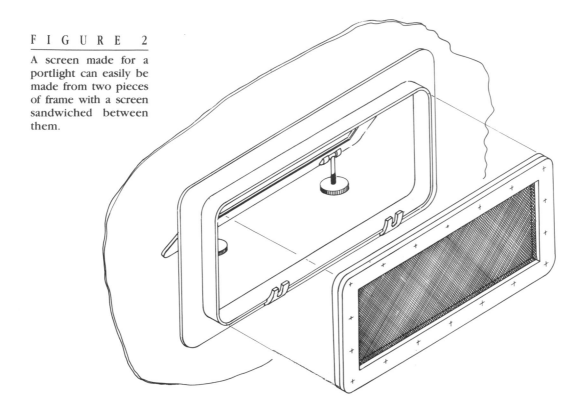

F I G U R E   2
A screen made for a portlight can easily be made from two pieces of frame with a screen sandwiched between them.

of two parts, which are screwed or bolted together to hold the screen in place. This method is often simpler than using a piece of quarter round to secure the screen. If you have access to a table saw, the screen casing can be made by temporarily clamping two pieces of plywood together and cutting out the required shape. This will ensure that both halves match.

A screen for the main companionway is always useful. It should be made to fit where the washboards are normally fitted and should be a little sturdier than the smaller screens. Also, an additional screen fitting horizontally over the top of the main hatch allows the hatch to be kept fully open for maximum ventilation.

In Figure 3 the screen rests on top of the open hatch. The reason for this is that quite often the screen is forgotten by a crewman climbing out of the hatch. If it sits on top of the hatch, the person climbing the companionway ladder will simply dislodge it without damaging it.

Figure 3A shows an exploded view of the hatch screen. It has a corner routed out to accept the screening material. The quarter round is then nailed in place to hold the screen in place. In Figure 3B the screened panel can be made to be

hinged, making it nonremovable. If you still want to have it be removable, you would have to use hinges with removable pins.

TO MAKE THE SCREEN

First carefully measure the opening you intend to screen and cut a cardboard template to an exact fit. Trim the cardboard where any protrusions or notches prevent the screen from fitting flush. To lay out the edge pieces, you can either make a new drawing of the screen or use the existing cardboard template. Once the measuring is done, assembly is straightforward. The corners are doweled and glued. Make sure the frame is laid flat and is square before the glue dries.

Once the frame is made, it should be varnished or painted before the screen is installed. Remember to varnish or paint the quarter-round pieces that hold the screen in place before installation. To install the screen, lay it over the frame and tack the quarter-round trim pieces in place. Make sure the screen material is tight, without stress lines. With the quarter-round pieces tacked in place, the screen material can be trimmed and the entire unit is ready for a final coat of paint or varnish.

F I G U R E   3

The companionway hatch screen should slide in where the washboards normally fit.

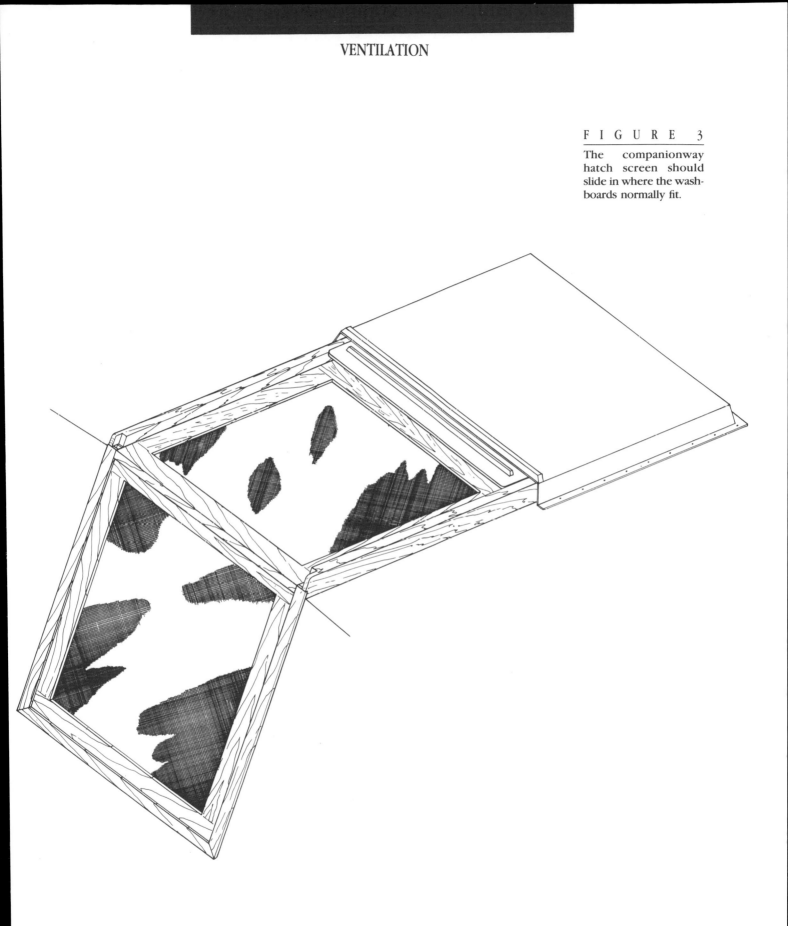

F I G U R E 3A

An exploded view of the hatch screen. Note the quarter round to hold the trim in place.

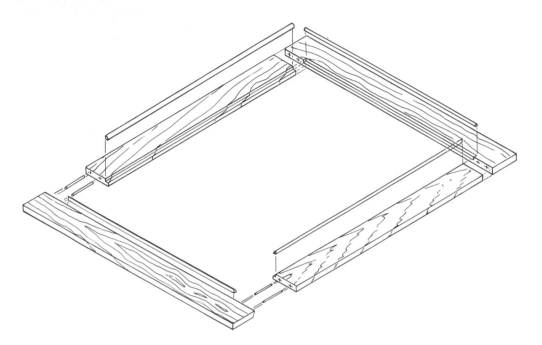

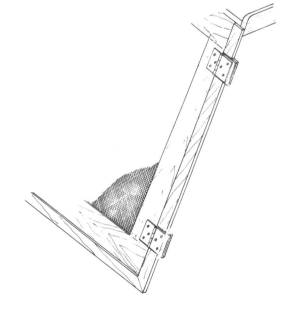

F I G U R E 3B

The screen could also be made to be hinged. Removing the hinge pins will enable the screen to be removed.

PROJECT 6 - 4
THE DORADE VENT

Suppose you need both light and ventilation down below. A simple method of getting both is to install a dorade vent with a Plexiglas top. Project 6-4 shows such a vent box. The ventilator part is easily purchased from Nicro Fico or other manufacturers (see Appendix for addresses). Let's suppose you have a 6-inch (150 mm) diameter ventilator (Nicro Fico part number NF 24206CH for the chrome on brass unit). You need a 6-inch (150 mm) diameter pipe to vent the air through the deck. This must be cut flush to the ceiling on the underside and at a 45-degree angle on the top. Three inches (75 mm) of pipe sticking up into the vent box will allow water to flow around the vent but not into the boat. (If you don't want to make the dorade box, Nicro Fico makes an entire 3- or 4-inch (75 mm or 100 mm) unit that can be easily bolted to the deck. Ask for part number NF 10917CH. Nicro Fico also makes insect screens for ventilators. Ask for part number NF 10953 for the 3-inch, NF 10954 for the 4-inch, and NF 10955 for the 5-inch screen.)

BUILDING THE VENT BOX

First mark the position of the vent on the deck and check that the deckhead is clear inside the boat. Marking the vent on the deck will also help you determine its size. In general a 6-inch (150 mm) diameter pipe will need 7 inches (175 mm) inside the box. Thus, if you are using ¾-inch (18 mm) wood for the vent box, you'll have an overall width of 8½ inches (216 mm). If you have two 6-inch (150 mm) holes in the dorade box and an inch at either end with a 2-inch space between them, the total length of the top of the vent box will be 16 inches. The front face can be any slope you desire; let's say it will be 60 degrees. With a height of 7 inches, this gives a total length of almost 20 inches. You can lay the dimensions out on a piece of teak or mahogany 7 or 8 inches (175 mm or 200 mm) wide.

Cut out the four pieces as shown in the exploded view, Figure 1. Remember that the front piece is slightly longer than the side pieces because it is sloped. Note also how the edges are rabbeted to make the joint stronger and to hide some of the end grain. Carefully cut the translucent or smoked plastic top to fit flush around the edges. (Do not use glass; it breaks too easily.) At this point the box can be glued and screwed together without the top. Figure 2 shows the dorade vent fully assembled.

MOUNTING

Once you have determined the position of the unit on the deck, remove the interior ceiling and drill a pilot hole where the tube to the interior will be fitted. Then cut this hole to as near the desired diameter as possible. Next locate and glue and screw to the deck the chocks at either end of the dorade box. (Marked C in Figure 3: The full-size section). Now install the deck tube. It should be fastened in place and caulked carefully so that no water can leak between it and the deck. (Note: If you have a cored deck, it may be desirable to seal the core material with resin or epoxy before installing the vent tube. This could prevent water migration into the core.)

With the tube in place and carefully caulked, it is time to install the vent box by screwing it to the blocks at C. You may want to add caulking around the edge of the box, but this is unnecessary, as the water should flow out.

With the box installed and the vent tube in place, all that remains is to mount the plastic cover and fit the ventilator. Some people like to pour a little water down the ventilator hole to make sure that the unit is watertight and that the drains work before bolting everything down tightly.

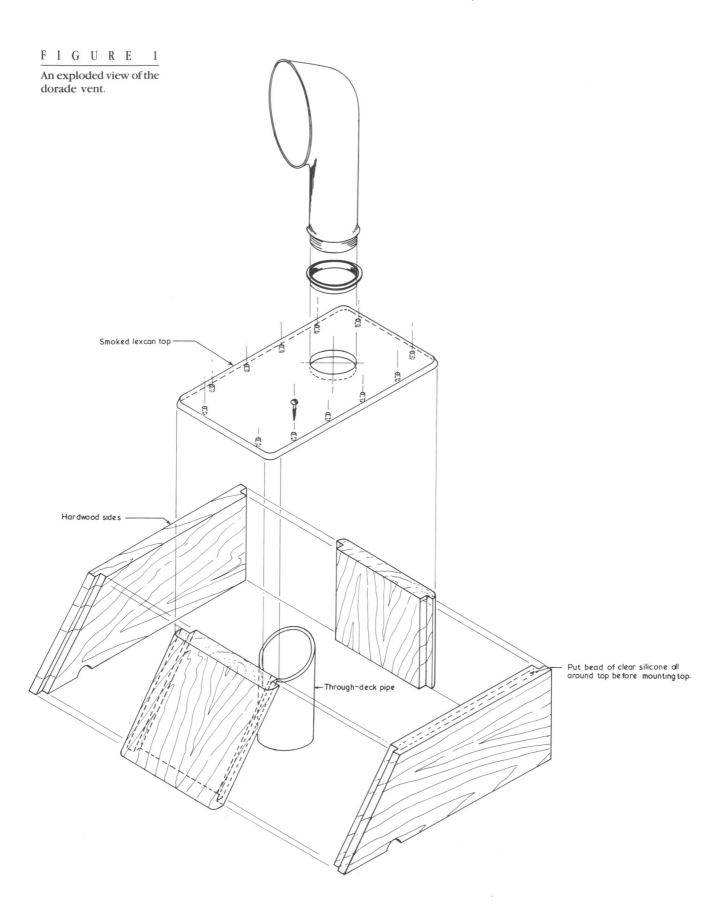

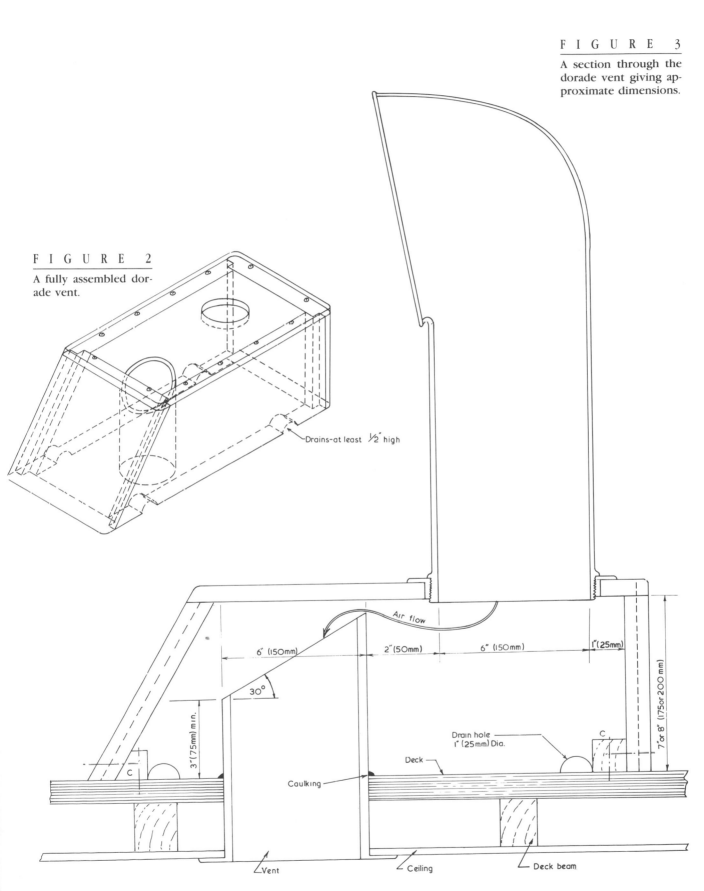

FIGURE 3
A section through the dorade vent giving approximate dimensions.

FIGURE 2
A fully assembled dorade vent.

Drains-at least ½" high

Air flow

6" (150mm) 2" (50mm) 6" (150mm) 1" (25mm)

30°

3" (75mm) min.

7" or 8" (175 or 200 mm)

C

Drain hole
1" (25mm) Dia.

C

Deck

Caulking

Vent

Ceiling

Deck beam

PROJECT 6 - 5
VENTILATING OTHER AREAS

The lazaret, galley, head, and other hard-to-vent areas need some special attention to make sure they get good airflow. It helps, when figuring out how to vent a compartment, to think about where the air can enter and how it can escape. Air has to be pulled, you cannot push it, so a fan must be placed at the downwind end of the system. Figure 1 shows part of a longitudinal section through a boat in way of the lazaret. If a louvered panel is inserted into the aft bulkhead and a vent installed in the afterdeck, smells will be drawn out of the inside of the vessel, through the lazaret, and into the air. Figure 7 shows how a vent should be installed. Follow the manufacturer's instructions to install this unit properly.

The galley is another area where both active and passive ventilation are required. Figure 2 shows where to site the vents in the galley for best results. There should be one over the stove, so that heat and cooking smells are pulled out of the interior, and another vent over the sink, to pull steam out. These need not be vents installed in the overhead. They can be installed in a locker and vented through the overhead using ducting. Figure 3 shows a typical layout.

You can use either a dorade vent or a solar vent (pictured in Figure 7) to improve airflow in most places. However, if you decide to install a dorade, make sure it does not foul any lines, winches, or cleats on deck if the galley is near the aft end of the cabin. This area is normally quite crowded. Sometimes a vent from the galley will emerge on deck under the dodger. If it does, heat and smells from the galley may be vented into the cockpit. By using a short piece of ducting, the solar vent or dorade can be placed almost anywhere on deck.

The head definitely needs a vent. In this case a fan, as shown in Figure 3, can be built into a locker, a solar vent or dorade installed in the overhead, or either can be installed in a portlight, as shown in Figure 4. While most manufacturers

F I G U R E 1

One of the areas that usually needs ventilating is the lazaret. By installing a louvered panel in the aft bulkhead and a vent on the afterdeck, satisfactory ventilation can be obtained.

F I G U R E 2

Galley ventilation is a major requirement on almost all boats. The ideal place for the installation of mechanically driven fans is over the stove and over the sink, as shown here.

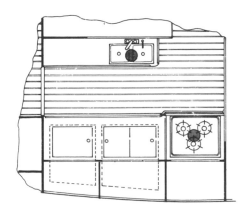

install a passive system, you might want to add an active unit. In this case a fan operated by a switch near the door would be ideal, or the solar vent will keep the head ventilated at all times. Either unit can be retrofitted in place of the existing vent. If you want to install a dorade vent but don't have the room, Nicro Fico and other companies make a vent that is completely self-contained. It allows air and water to enter the top, but the water is drained out the side and the air enters the boat. It is designed to fit into a round hole that the cowl normally fits in without having to make a complete box. This would be ideal in the position shown in Figure 4.

Finally, if you are going to build a metal boat, you might want to include a passive system in the construction. This system, shown in Figures 5 and 6, has a number of slots cut in the bow. Air flows through these slots and water drains from the drain hole. You will probably have to install a fan to pull air into the interior of the boat. Of if you have a solar vent installed aft, it will draw the air into the interior via the louvered panel in the upper part of the watertight bulkhead, as shown in Figure 6. Remember, though, if you intend to install this type of system, all bulkheads or doors should have louvered panels to allow complete air circulation throughout the boat.

F I G U R E 3

A fan need not be mounted directly over the area to be vented. It can be mounted in a locker and ducting used to channel the air out.

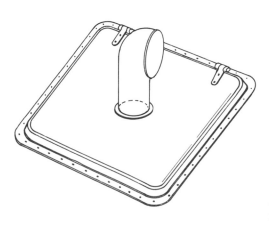

F I G U R E 4

Often a simple solution to ventilation problems is to install a dorade type directly in a hatch, as shown.

FIGURE 5

If you are having a metal boat built, a ventilation system can be built into the boat quite simply. Here vents in the bow allow air to enter. The vented bulkhead allows air to pass through while water drains out of the drain holes provided.

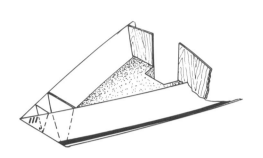

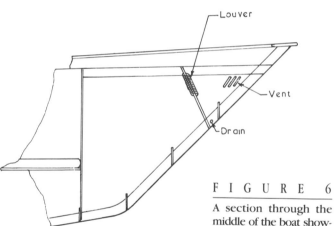

FIGURE 6

A section through the middle of the boat showing details of the bow ventilation system. Note the louvered vent situated high on the bulkhead and the drain hole.

FIGURE 7

A Nicro Fico solar-powered ventilator installed in a hatch (photo courtesy of Nicro Fico Corp.).

CHAPTER 7

DAVITS AND DINGHIES

One of the most vexing questions for many boat owners is where to store the dinghy. Often the cabin top is too small for the dinghy, and putting it on the foredeck makes sail handling very difficult. The solution on boats with sufficient freeboard is to put it on davits.

PROJECT 7-1
DAVITS

Figure 1 shows simple wooden davits you can build yourself. They do have a drawback, however. When the dinghy is stowed on the davits and the boat motored at moderate speeds, the stern wave may hit the dinghy, running the risk of knocking it and the davits off the boat. Having given this warning, the method of constructing these davits is shown in Figure 2. Each davit is a simple tapered wooden beam with a sheave or tackle at the outboard end. The line is fastened to the underside of the davit and is taken around a block before running back over the sheave in the davit to get a 2-to-1 purchase. Fasten it to a becket on the block and fit a pair of sheaves in the davit to get a 3-to-1 purchase. This line is then taken to a cleat to secure the dinghy. Note that you may require a chock at position A in Figure 1 to enable the dinghy to be cinched up tight to the davit.

Figure 3 shows a commercially purchased set of davits. Simpson Lawrence makes them for sail and power yachts. They are relatively easy to install by following the manufacturer's instructions.

If you can stow your dinghy on the cabin top or on deck but have trouble launching it, Figure 4 may show a solution. It is a removable davit. The davit is made from pipe sufficiently strong to support the dinghy. When not in use, it is stored flat on deck in chocks made to suit it. When in use, the davit fits into a bracket mounted against the bulwark, as shown in Figure 6. It drops into the bracket and is held in place by the small boss at A. The bearing welded on the bottom makes it easy for the davit to be turned when the dinghy has been hoisted. A cleat should be welded to the davit to belay the hoisting line. Note also that the bracket should be through-bolted to a deck beam or other strong point below deck.

This removable davit has more than one use. It can be used to lift heavy stores out of the dinghy, or if a second bracket is placed forward, it can serve as an anchor davit to keep a Fisherman anchor away from the side of the boat, as shown in Figure 5.

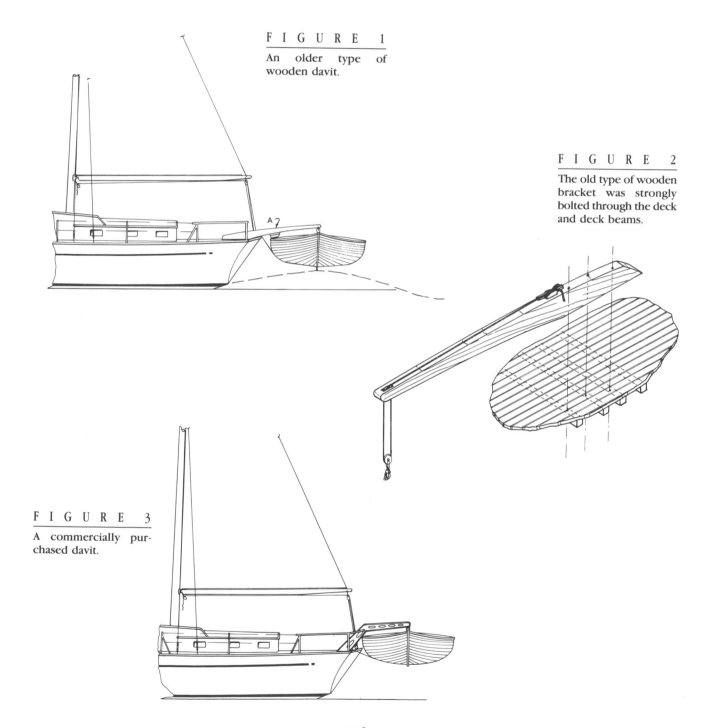

FIGURE 1
An older type of wooden davit.

FIGURE 2
The old type of wooden bracket was strongly bolted through the deck and deck beams.

FIGURE 3
A commercially purchased davit.

F I G U R E 4

If the dinghy is to be stowed on a cabin top, then this removable davit may be the easy way to get it there.

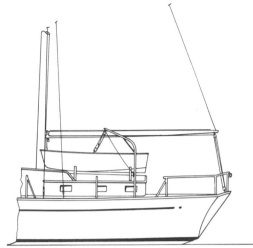

F I G U R E 6

The bracket for the pipe davit can be made out of steel or brass and bolted in place.

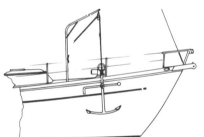

F I G U R E 5

With the addition of a second bracket forward, the davit can be used to lift the Fisherman anchor aboard.

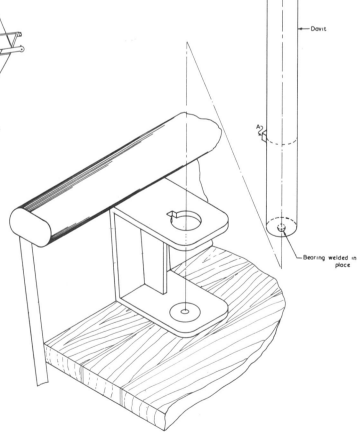

PROJECT 7-2
A PLYWOOD DINGHY: THE HULL

To round out this book, here's a simple plywood dinghy that the kids can have fun with at the boat, beach, or lake. Note that two versions can be built, one with simple bench seats and the other with foam-filled, sealed compartment seats for additional bouyancy, as shown in Project 7-4. I strongly advise that the version with built-in bouyancy be built. While it has less volume than the other version, it should stay afloat even when swamped if a high-density foam is used in the end compartments. Note also that any children playing with this dinghy should always be wearing life preservers.

With these cautions given, let's look at the dinghy. It is made from sheet plywood and is designed to be fitted together easily. There are two methods of holding the plywood together. The first is to stitch the pieces together with copper wire and then tape all the seams with fiberglass tape. The second is to fit battens in the corners and screw the pieces to the battens. The seams are then taped over.

Figure 1 shows the sections through the dinghy. As you can see, it is flat-bottomed for ease of hauling ashore and has boxy, vertical sides. Figure 2 shows the layout using removable seats if you desire to keep the bottom open. The seats merely rest on the side pieces.

CUTTING OUT THE PARTS

It will take two sheets of ½-inch-thick (12 mm) plywood 4' × 8' (1.22 m × 2.44 m) to build this dinghy. The pieces are laid out as shown in Figure 3. On the second sheet (not shown) you will cut out two more side pieces and use the remainder for the rudder blade, daggerboard, and end compartments. Full-size templates for these pieces and complete plans for the dinghy are available from Cruising Craft Inc. (see Appendix for address) at a cost of $35.00.

STITCHING AND GLUING

When all the pieces have been cut out, they need to be glued together. If you choose to use the stitch-and-glue method, you will have to drill small holes the diameter of the wire you intend to use along each side. Copper wire is very malleable and can be cut and twisted easily. You should probably use wire about ³⁄₃₂ inch (2.5 mm) in diameter. Starting at the

F I G U R E   1

The sections of the 6 cc dinghy.

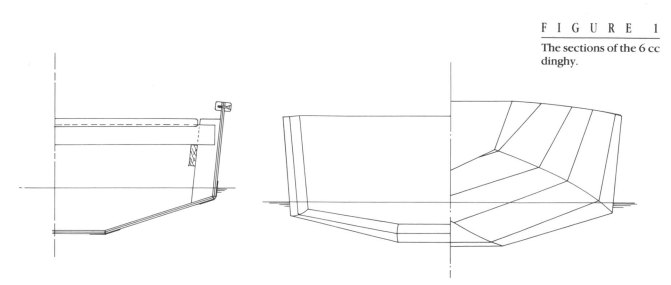

bow, drill two small holes opposite each other, insert the wire, pull it tight, and twist the ends together. Cut the twist off fairly short (but not so short that it will undo) and fold it against the hull. Repeat this procedure every 6 inches (150 mm), adding more stitches where the sides don't quite meet.

When all the sides are held together tightly, you can start taping the seams. Use fiberglass tape either 3″ or 4″ (75 or 100 mm) wide and polyester resin to fix in place. If you build

the dinghy upside down, twist the stiches on the inside. The tape can then be applied on the outside of the hull. When the two layers are dry, the wires can be cut and pulled out. Now the dinghy can be turned over and the inside joints thoroughly taped. Next make the parts for the bouyancy compartments as described in Project 7-4. Fit them tightly, fill with foam, and tape the joints carefully.

F I G U R E   2

The dinghy is assembled using the stitch-and-glue method. Seats are optional.

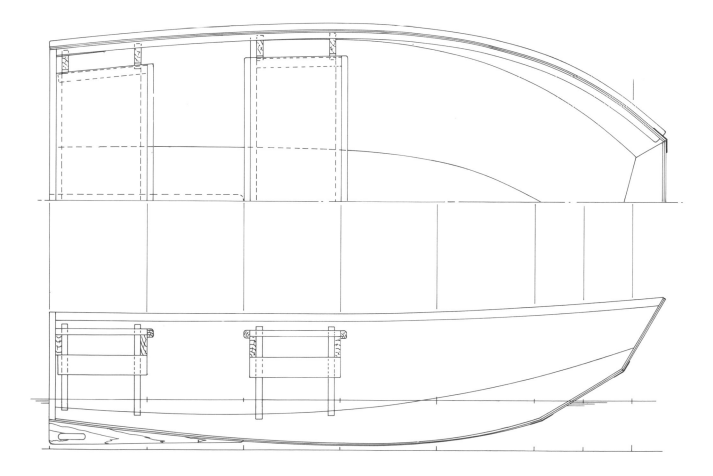

PARTS LIST

ITEM	SIZE (IN INCHES)	HOW MUCH?
⅜-inch marine-grade plywood	8′ × 4′	2 sheets
Fiberglass tape	4″	90′
Hardwood	¾″ × 1″	30′
Flathead wood screws	1½″, #8	30
Copper wire	#10 or #12	50′
Hardwood for skeg	1½″ × 3½″	2′
Softwood for oarlock pads	¾″ × 5½″	4′
Bolts with nuts and washers	2″, #8	8
Epoxy resin with hardener	1 gall (approx.)	——

OPTIONAL TRANSOM AND BOTTOM

¾-inch marine-grade plywood	Part sheet	——
Hardwood	1½″ × ¾″	8′
Fiberglass tape	8″	12′

SEATS

Softwood	¾″ × 2½″	24′
Softwood	¾″ × 11½″ or 11¾″	6′
Marine-grade plywood with ¾″ × ¾″ half round edging		
Bronze nails (or galvanized)	1½″	40
Waterproof glue	8 oz. (approx.)	——

PAINTING

Undercoat in desired color	1 gal. (approx.)
Topcoat in desired color	1 gal. (approx.)

Note: Wood sizes given as true dimension. For example, a 2-inch by 4-inch measures 3½ inches by 1½ inches true.

SUNDRIES

Filler
Sandpaper
Wood for forms

Spars are not listed here but may be added. (Make to the details shown
   on the plans.)

PARTS REQUIRED

Mast—2-inch-diameter post, 7 feet long
Booms—1-inch-diameter dowel, 11 feet long
Use seat parts list to make mast support seat

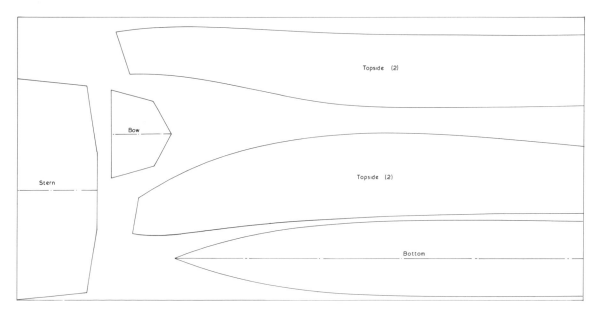

FIGURE 3
The various parts of the
dinghy fit on two sheets
of plywood. Bow, stern,
bottom, and two sides
are laid out here.

PROJECT 7 - 3
FITTING OUT THE DINGHY

The dinghy should be floatable at this stage, but if you build the sailing version, it will require a rudder and daggerboard, as shown in Figure 1. Both boards are made from two pieces of plywood glued together and shaped as shown.

The mast is fastened to the forward transverse bulkhead as shown in Figure 2 and the simple lugsail rig is supported on wooden spars that are sized as shown in Figure 3.

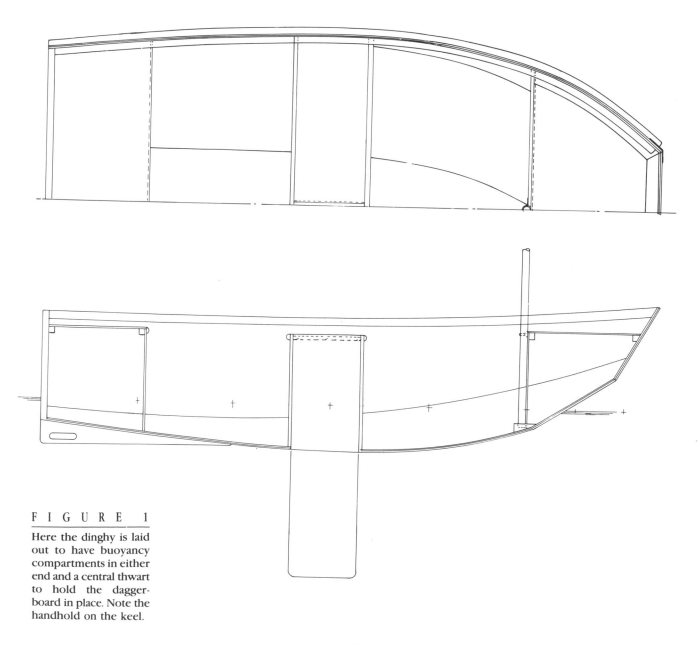

Here the dinghy is laid out to have buoyancy compartments in either end and a central thwart to hold the daggerboard in place. Note the handhold on the keel.

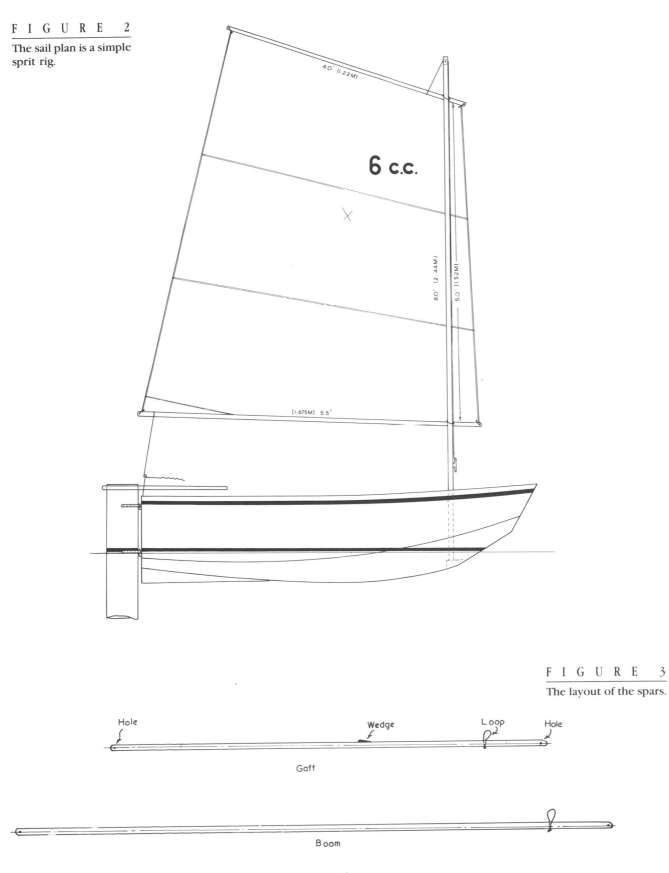

The sail plan is a simple sprit rig.

4.0˚ (1.2 2M)

6 c.c.

8.0˚ (2.44M)

5.0˚ (1.52M)

[1.675M] 5.5´

F I G U R E   3

The layout of the spars.

Hole   Wedge   Loop   Hole

Gaff

Boom

163

P R O J E C T   7 - 4
A FOAM-CORED DINGHY

If you intend to build a foam-cored yacht, it will be good practice to build a foam-cored dinghy first. This will enable you to practice the techniques and solve any minor problems before you get into a major project. Here is a simple yacht tender that can be built by an amateur in a garage. Figure 1 shows the lines of the craft; note how simple they are. The rounded bow makes it easy to come alongside without gouging the topsides.

Figure 2 shows the sail plan and deck layout. The seats at either end are simply blocks of foam carved to shape and glassed in place. This will provide some bouyancy for the boat. The central thwart provides support for the dagger-board and is also used as a thwart when rowing. There is a skeg on the bottom of the boat for grounding and handling when the dinghy is upside down. Note also that skids can be installed if the dinghy is to be dragged up and down beaches.

F I G U R E   1

The lines plan of the dinghy.

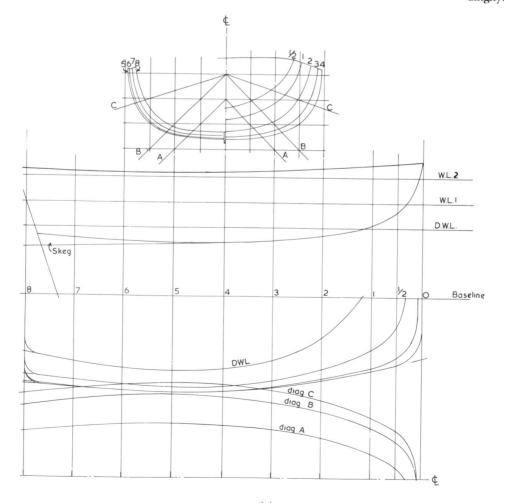

F I G U R E   2

F I G U R E   2

The arrangement plan. Note the foam-filled seats for extra buoyancy and the simple sprit rig.

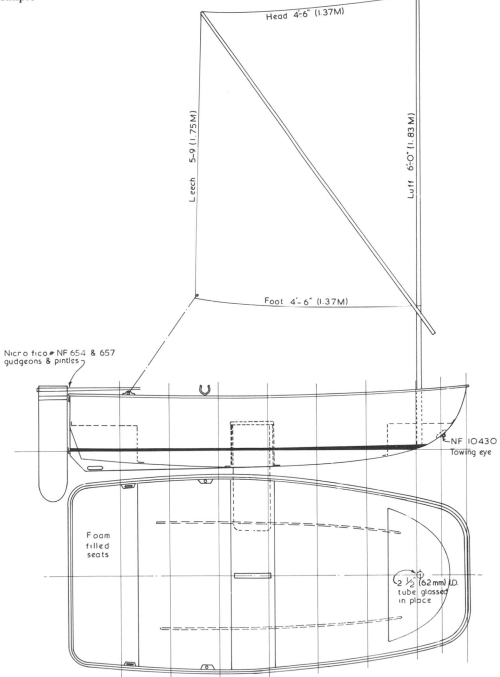

Head 4'-6" (1.37M)

Leech 5'-9 (1.75M)

Luff 6'-0" (1.83M)

Foot 4'-6" (1.37M)

Nicro fico# NF 654 & 657 gudgeons & pintles

NF 10430 Towing eye

Foam filled seats

2 ½" (62 mm) I.D. tube glassed in place

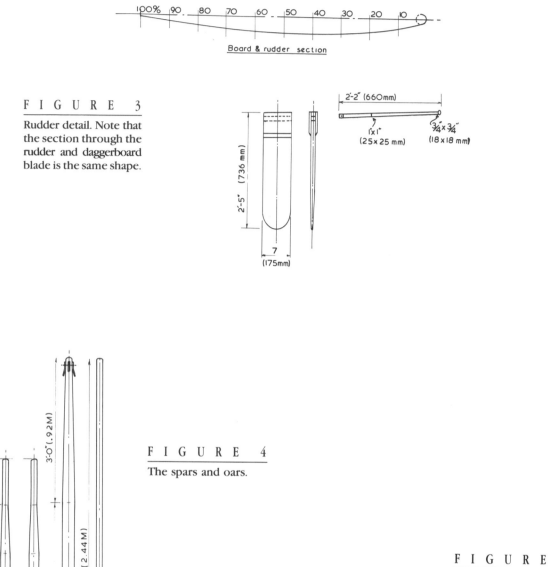

Board & rudder section

F I G U R E 3

Rudder detail. Note that the section through the rudder and daggerboard blade is the same shape.

2'-2" (660mm)

1"x1" (25 x 25 mm)

¾"x¾" (18 x 18 mm)

2'-5" (736 mm)

7 (175mm)

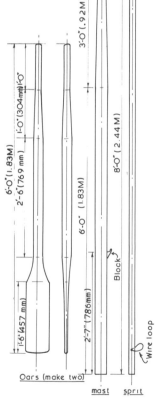

3'-0" (.9 2M)

6'-0" (1.83M)

1'-0" (304mm) 1'-0"

2'-6" (769 mm)

8'-0" (2.44 M)

6'-0" (1.83M)

1'-6" (457 mm)

2'-7" (786mm)

Block

Wire loop

Oars (make two)

mast   sprit

F I G U R E 4

The spars and oars.

F I G U R E 5

Cut the sections out of plywood ready for mounting on the strongback.

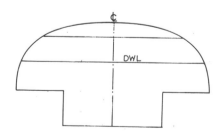

℄

DWL

166

The sheerline has a rubrail around it that is carefully screwed to the hull. The sail plan is a simple sprit rig that may be adjusted by the mainsheet attached to the transom. Should there be a problem with helm balance, then the mast can be moved to the aft end of the forward platform rather than being located in a hole in the middle of the thwart.

Figure 3 shows the layout of the rudder and daggerboard. Both are made of ¾-inch (18 mm) plywood shaped as shown. The rudder has a parabolic tip, but the daggerboard will move around in the slot when it is raised if it is given the same tip. For this reason the daggerboard has a square tip.

Figure 4 shows the layout of the spars. This should be straightforward. Use pine or spruce for spars.

BUILDING THE DINGHY

Maybe you want to build your own boat. If you do, you should try a simpler project to get the building techniques organized and figure out the amount of work involved. This dinghy is an ideal project to enable you to organize the work.

First you will need to lay the full-size section out on ½-inch (12 mm) plywood sheets to make up your plug. Full-size sections are available from Cruising Craft Inc. (see Appendix), or you can scale the drawings up from this book. You can do this in one of two ways; either lay out each section on a piece of paper and glue the paper to the plywood or lay out each section directly onto the plywood. Remember that the lines plan only shows one side of the hull, and you will need to make two sides and butt them together in the middle. Figure 5 shows how a typical section should look before it is mounted on the strongback.

To make the strongback, use two pieces of 2-inch by 6-inch (50-mm × 150-mm) lumber 10 feet (3.04 m) long. Mark the lumber at 1 foot (305 mm) and carefully cut 8 pieces of 2 × 6 inch (50 mm × 150 mm) lumber 24 inches (610 mm) long. Use these pieces to make a frame as shown in Figure 6. Make sure that the frame is perfectly level. Adjust the height by shimming the corners as required with wedges. Some builders glue the frame to the working floor with a pat of epoxy putty to prevent it moving or twisting. If you nail a vertical piece of wood at each end and stretch a taut wire between them, this will give you a centerline on which all the sections can be set up.

Now set each section up on the frame as shown in Figure 6. Make sure the centerlines are lined up on the centerline wire and adjust each section vertically until all the waterlines are perfectly aligned.

At this stage you will need to add an extra piece at each end of the plug to make the compound curves easy to fabricate. Figure 7 shows the shape of the pieces for the stern area. At this stage the plug is ready to receive the longitudinal battens. These are best if they are notched into the sections. If you cut the battens to fit between the sections, they will not assume the correct curvature and the boat will have many bumps and hollows. The battens should be spaced about 6 to 8 inches (150 to 200 mm) apart and run from stem to stern. Figure 8 shows what the mold should look like at this stage.

Now we are ready to lay the foam over the mold. Use contoured foam or balsa core and sew it to the longitudinals. You will only need a stitch about every 6 inches (150 mm). Make sure that the foam lies smoothly on the mold and that the edges butt properly. Adjust the foam until the entire surface of the boat is smooth, without any hollows or bumps. You may find that you have to use a little epoxy glue to ensure that the edges of the foam join perfectly, but getting the working surface perfectly smooth now will save hours of work later. You can also nail the foam to the longitudinals with finish nails, but this method often disturbs the panels already set in place.

Make the transom from ½-inch (12 mm) plywood, as it may be fitted with a small (not more than 3 hp) outboard. You may find that you need to double up the plywood in way of the outboard bracket but ½ inch (12 mm) ply should suffice if a small outboard is used. Now brush off all the dust and clean up the working area. You are ready to lay the fiberglass over the mold. To apply the fiberglass, drape a strip over the hull from sheerline to sheerline and cut it to size, leaving an inch or two (25 or 50 mm) around the sheer. Most builders lay the glass on the diagonal to get long pieces and greatest rigidity. Lay a second piece next to it and trim as before. Some builders like to overlap the glass, but that will leave a bump, others butt the ends of the glass and use the second or third layers to maintain strength. Now mix the

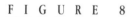

F I G U R E   7

The ends of the dinghy will have to be made from scraps of plywood cut to suit the shape.

F I G U R E   6

Mount the sections on the strongback as shown here. Make sure that the frame is perfectly level and well supported.

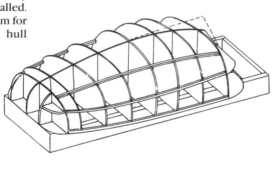

F I G U R E   8

The finished mold ready for foam to be installed. Use contoured foam for the smoothest hull shape.

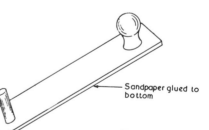

Sandpaper glued to bottom

F I G U R E   9

A longboard can easily be made from scraps of plywood, and with sandpaper glued lightly to the bottom, it can be used for sanding the hull of the dinghy.

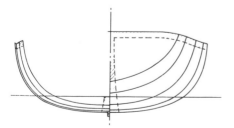

F I G U R E   10

Strip the foam away from the shaded areas and apply the inner laminate.

resin according to the manufacturer's instructions. Pour some of the wet resin onto the fiberglass and roll it out carefully. Make sure that you get good penetration through the glass —in other words, that the glass is thoroughly wetted out. Lay more glass on the mold and wet it out until the entire foam layer is covered with fiberglass. You can let it dry, but you will need to clean the surface before laying on the next layer of glass and resin, so most builders keep on working. The second layer should be installed on the opposite diagonal to the first. It can be draped carefully over the first layer and wetted out as before. Finally the third layer should be installed and the entire hull left to cure. This will take 3 days to 2 weeks, depending upon humidity and temperature.

A word of warning:

1. The resin will give off heat as it cures. Make sure used pots of resin are disposed of carefully.
2. Some people are sensitive to polyester resin. Use rubber gloves and a barrier cream to make sure you are well protected. Use throwaway overalls or old clothes when laying up fiberglass.
3. Use adequate ventilation. The fumes given off from some types of resin can be highly toxic.
4. Do not smoke while laying up fiberglass.

When the hull is cured, it is time to start work again. First grind off the highest bumps, taking care not to go through any of the laminate. Now fill the hollows with filler. You can use expensive epoxy resin with micro baloons or the less-expensive car-body filler; they do the job equally well. Carefully grind off the high spots and fill the low spots until the entire hull is perfectly fair. Use a long batten to find the hollows and humps. Lay the batten over the hull and move it around, looking under it to find voids or bumps. Mark them carefully and either fill or grind them off until the hull is smooth. The final grinding should be done with a longboard as shown in Figure 9. A trick here is to apply different colors of filler in separate layers, then you will be able to see where bumps and hollows are located. The last layers will probably

have to be sprayed on and sanded until the hull is perfectly fair. You can skip this stage if you are satisfied with a slightly lower standard. Finally spray on the undercoat and the dinghy is ready to be turned over.

You should now make up a cradle to fit the bottom of the dinghy. A trick here is to lay a piece of plastic over the hull, securing it carefully at both ends to the strongback. Now lay a few strips of fiberglass on the plastic and wet them out. Lay a piece of plywood vertically on top of the wetted-out glass and glass the plywood to the strips laid over the hull. When they cure, you will have a perfect cradle to hold the dinghy when it is turned over. After curing, remove the strips and build a solid cradle. Now turn the entire dinghy and strongback over, placing it carefully in the cradle. Cut the sewing, holding the foam to the mold, and remove the mold. You should have a clean, slightly rubbery, dinghy ready for the inside laminate to be installed.

Now lay up the interior laminate, using the same technique as for the exterior layers. Note that you should cut away the core material near the sheer, as shown in Figure 10. Laminate up to and just beyond the sheerline. Let them cure. When the hull has cured, you can fair up the inside. This need not be done as smoothly as the exterior. Also trim off excess glass around the sheerline and fill any voids. The interior should be smooth enough so that you can walk on it in bare feet, as you probably will do in summer. This is the basic hull construction completed.

Now you should make the bow and stern seats. Either make them out of scrap plywood and glass in place or carve a solid block of foam to fit and glass it in place. In both cases the seats should be fully encapsulated. If you like, you can add a varnished seat cover to give a pleasing appearance, but remember to paint the boat, inside and out, before installing the wooden seats or wooden rubrail.

Make the daggerboard and wrap it in plastic. Lay up the daggerboard trunk around the board, making sure the trunk is high enough to come to the top of the middle seat. When the trunk has cured, remove the plastic and make sure the board slides easily. The thwart in the middle of the boat is made the same way as the end boxes, either by fabricating out of plywood or foam. Fit the thwart, its supports, and the foam around the daggerboard and glass the entire assembly

169

in place. Cut the slot for the board in the bottom of the dinghy and seal the edges with resin. Cap the thwart with a varnished wooden seat.

Around the sheerline you have several options. Two wooden half round strips will give a satisfactory rail, especially if the wood matches the thwarts. Or you can use a rubber or metal caprail; most are simply bolted in place. Follow the manufacturer's instructions for best results.

The rudder should be fitted as shown in Figure 2. It hangs on gudgeons and pins obtainable from Nicro Fico. (See Appendix for address). Now make the spars as shown in Figure 4. They should be fitted carefully as shown in Figure 3. If you like, you can ignore the spars and make a pair of oars for rowing the dinghy, or forget both oars and the daggerboard and put a small outboard on the transom. No more than a 3-horsepower motor should be used; a trolling motor would be ideal.

Now the boat is ready for sea trials. Remember to wear a lifejacket. And have fun!

PARTS LIST

You will require approximately the following amounts to construct this dinghy:

> About 22 yards of 1½-ounce (39 gm/m²) chopped-strand mat (C.S.M.)
> About 12 yards of 10-ounce (260 gm/m²) woven roving (W.R.)
> 4 or 5 sheets of core material
> About 2 to 3 gallons (1–2 Kgs) of resin

These amounts are for the hull only and will vary according to the way the materials are cut. The actual resin content will vary according to the lay-up, but you should try to get a 35 percent glass-to-resin ratio.

You will also need wood for the strongback, one or two sheets of plywood for the sections, and about 60 feet of battens and pine for oars and spars.

MINIMUM HULL LAMINATE

Outside laminate: 1 layer 1½-ounce C.S.M.
1 layer 10-ounce W.R.
1 layer 1½-ounce C.S.M.
Core material: ½-inch Klegecell, Divynicell, Airex, or balsa
Inside laminate: 1 layer 1½-ounce C.S.M.
1 layer 10-ounce W.R.
1 layer 1½-ounce C.S.M. (Optional)

APPENDIX: LIST OF MANUFACTURERS MENTIONED
IN THE TEXT

Harken,
1251 East Wisconsin Avenue,
Pewaukee, Wisconsin 53702
Nicro Corp.,
2065 West Avenue 140th,
San Leandro, California 94577
The Edson Corp.,
460 Industrial Park Road,
New Bedford, Massachusetts 02745
Cruising Craft Inc.,
P.O. Box 335
Jamestown, Rhode Island 02835
Simpson Lawrence, Ltd.
218/228 Edmiston Drive
Glasgow, Scotland G51 2YT